MR. SELFRIDGE
IN CHICAGO

D1596679

GAYLE SOUCEK

MR. SELFRIDGE
IN CHICAGO

MARSHALL FIELD'S,
THE WINDY CITY
& THE MAKING OF A
MERCHANT PRINCE

THE
History
PRESS

Published by The History Press
Charleston, SC
www.historypress.net

All images from author's collection unless otherwise noted.

First published 2015

Manufactured in the United States

ISBN 978.1.62619.736.7

Library of Congress Control Number: 2015937994

Contents

Introduction

Nothing in the world is done as well as it can be done.
—Harry Gordon Selfridge

History is always a bit of a puzzle. Faded dates inscribed in yellowed ledgers, names spelled incorrectly in elaborate and hard-to-decipher script, carefully recorded but distorted memories of survivors…no amount of research can ever claim to portray events of the distant past with 100 percent accuracy. The best that an author can do is to review multiple sources of information and attempt to glean that tiny common thread that most likely hints at the real truth. You might find that some small bits of information in this book conflict with other sources, but rest assured that each conclusion drawn was the result of lengthy investigation and careful study.

Harry Gordon Selfridge presents an extraordinary enigma—the poor Wisconsin lad who honed his trade among Chicago's (indeed, the world's) most celebrated merchants before he headed off to take London by storm. Much of his early and rather unremarkable life went unrecorded, only to be reinvented and colorized at Harry's whims. He would brazenly shave years off his age to the extent that even his wife and children were uncertain of his true birth date. Some tales he told were true, others were embellished and some were blatant pants-on-fire fabrications. In fact, it sometimes seems that there were two Harrys: the talented and hardworking merchant whose story was reported in Chicago and the regal British Harry, whose exaggerated recollections of his earlier years often differ sharply from past chronicles.

Perhaps he felt the need to dramatize his circumstances because to Harry, good was never good enough. Everything in his world needed to be spectacular, larger than life. In many ways, this trait served him well. Because he aimed so high, he achieved more than most of his peers. However, this pursuit of excesses also proved to be his downfall. One thing can be said for certain: Harry Gordon Selfridge was a man who lived to his fullest capacity and changed the lives of those who surrounded him in the process. He was a showman, a magician and, perhaps, in the end, just a hungry boy who wanted to make his mother proud.

The Humble Beginnings

It is not the making of money that is the chief motive with me. It is the great game that is the thing.

—Harry Gordon Selfridge

Ripon, Wisconsin, is a small midwestern town that has birthed some very big ideas. Situated on the gentle rolling hills and meadows of the upper Fox River basin in Wisconsin—about eighty-five miles northwest of Milwaukee—the land once belonged to the American Indian tribes that fished its streams and hunted its woodlands. The Winnebagos, the Illinois, the Kickapoos, the Foxes, the Miamis and the gentle Mascoutins all lived in relative harmony. In fact, long before the white man arrived, there existed a massive Mascoutin village located just northwest of Ripon that housed more than twenty thousand individuals from five different tribes. They had come together to live in peace and in common defense against attacks by the warlike Iroquois, but as it turned out, the Iroquois were the least of their problems. French explorers convinced the Mascoutin people to resettle near the French fort at Detroit, where the peaceful tribe was systematically exterminated by the white conquerors and their Indian allies. By the mid-1800s, the remaining Fox Valley tribes were being forced from their lands under the Indian Removal Act of 1830 in order to make way for the European pioneers who were fast arriving to start a new life in the American frontier.

The first white men to settle permanently in the area arrived in May 1844. Nineteen men and one boy traveled from the town of Southport—

now Kenosha—to break ground for a grand social experiment. Known as the Wisconsin Phalanx, this group dreamed of creating an agricultural commune based on the teachings of French philosopher and socialist Charles Fourier. They named the community Ceresco in honor of Ceres, the Roman goddess of agriculture, and at its peak, about two hundred residents lived and worked cooperatively to farm its two thousand acres. Unlike some other utopian communitarian societies of the day, Ceresco carried little debt, and its assets exceeded its liabilities. Unfortunately, its financial success did little to quell the discontent of members who were growing tired of the cramped shared quarters and loss of autonomy. Slowly, the membership began to decline, and by 1849, it had become clear that the experiment was reaching an inevitable end. Over the next few years, the association sold off all of its land and other assets, and the money was divided equally among its shareholding members.

As the Ceresco commune began to liquidate, David Mapes, a steamboat captain from New York, arrived in search of land. Mapes had recently suffered the loss of his ship—and his livelihood as well—when the uninsured vessel sank after a collision. He took the meager salvage money and headed west without a firm plan in mind. Mapes recorded his adventures and explained why he came to Wisconsin: "I took another start in life and tried to acquire property which would not sink when having a hole stove in it." When he reached the Fox Valley, he was immediately dazzled by the beauty of the area. "Here for the first time in my life I saw a prairie…that prairie was the loveliest sight I had ever seen in nature, and through the summer with its monthly change of flowers, there was nothing more enchanting." Without hesitation, he returned to New York, packed up his family and belongings and headed back to the Wisconsin frontier to build a new home.

After a brief stint at farming, Mapes dreamed of building a city on the land, which he referred to as "a spot which was, in its state of nature, the fitting center of that Garden of Eden." At the time, most of the land adjacent to Ceresco was owned by Governor John Scott Horner. Horner agreed to sell the property, but with a few conditions. Among them, Mapes would have to build a gristmill and a public house, live in the town for at least one year and allow Horner to name the new city. Mapes agreed, and Ripon was born. It took its name from the picturesque ancient British cathedral city located on the River Ure in North Yorkshire, which was Horner's ancestral home. The town grew quickly and soon boasted a gristmill, a post office, a hotel, a blacksmith shop, a school and several stores. Finally, in 1853, Ceresco and Ripon were formally merged by the Wisconsin legislature. Although the lawmakers named the new town Morena, the name never stuck, and it was eventually incorporated as the city of Ripon.

By 1854, rumblings of discontent had begun to spread across the land as the issue of slavery was hotly debated between states. A group of alarmed citizens in Ripon convened at the local schoolhouse to discuss the implications of the Kansas-Nebraska Act, which had effectively overturned the 1820 Missouri Compromise and opened the door for the spread of slavery in the states. Fed up by what they considered a betrayal on the part of the current lawmakers, the Ripon folks decided that the time had come to create a new political party. They would call themselves "Republicans" in a nod to Thomas Jefferson's republican ideology.

The main focus of the group was to fight slavery, which they considered both a moral and an economic evil. Under the southern plantation system, a slave owner could buy up all the good land and inexpensively farm vast acreages by simply acquiring the needed number of slaves. An independent farmer who found the idea of human bondage abhorrent was limited to smaller, usually less desirable parcels that could realistically be worked by his own labor, perhaps with the help of family. As such, the plantation owners controlled the majority of the wealth and resources in the South. The northern abolitionists vowed to fight for "free labor, free land, and free men," which meant a return to individual effort and industry and an end to the slave trade. By 1860, the Republican Party that had formed just six years earlier in Ripon controlled Congress and most

Robert Oliver Selfridge, Harry's father, never returned to the family after his discharge from Civil War service. *Courtesy of Ripon Historical Society.*

of the northern states and had elected its first president, Abraham Lincoln. But by 1861, President Lincoln found himself at the helm of a gravely divided country spiraling into a bloody civil war. Many men left to fight, never to return home alive. Small-town cemeteries across the land marked the grim tally with their chiseled headstones.

One of Ripon's leading citizens—a dry goods merchant by the name of Robert Oliver Selfridge—was among those who left to go fight the Union's cause. Robert Oliver had settled in Ripon about a decade earlier in the 1850s along with his grandmother, father John and sister Martha. It appears that John later moved to Michigan, but young Robert and Martha stayed behind. Martha married a Ripon man named Edward Smith, and in 1853, Robert married a feisty young woman from Tecumseh, Michigan, named Lois Frances Baxter. He was thirty-one, and she was just eighteen. The newlyweds settled into a white frame cottage at the corner of Watson and Seward Streets in Ripon. Life seemed to be good for the Selfridges; Robert opened a small store right on the town square, and Lois stayed home to raise the couple's three boys. Birth records don't exist for the children and anecdotal family history is sketchy, but it appears likely that the oldest was Robert Oliver Jr., born in 1854. Charles Johnston was born in 1855, and the youngest—Henry (Harry) Gordon—was born on January 11, 1856. Most sources claim that Charles was the firstborn and Harry the middle child, but baptism records for the boys seem to indicate otherwise. It should also be noted that when Harry reached adulthood, he would routinely shave years off his age, so some resources list his birth year as late as 1866, but most reliable accounts place it as 1856.

Robert was active in the town, and according to an article in the *Ripon Commonwealth*, he enjoyed "a wide circle of friends and acquaintances." A devoted freemason, he soon became Master of Ripon Lodge No. 95. At some point, Robert closed his store, most likely due to the severe recession that began in 1856. He worked for a few years as a contractor in Ripon, but as the war began to brew in earnest, he moved his family to Michigan to be closer to other relatives. It was here in 1861 that he enlisted in the Third Michigan Calvary, leaving Lois and the boys in Tecumseh. Shortly thereafter, tragedy struck. Although there's no reliable record of the cause or the exact year, both Charles and Robert Jr. died within a short period, leaving Harry as an only child. Grieving, alone and with a small child to care for, Lois moved to Jackson, Michigan, and found a job teaching at West Grammar Grade School for thirty dollars per month. The salary was paltry, but it provided for a bare minimum of food and shelter. To add a few extra

In this photo of the town of Ripon, Wisconsin, Harry Gordon Selfridge's early childhood home can be seen—he and his brothers were born in the white cottage with the long sloping roof at the far right of the photo. *Courtesy of Ripon Historical Society.*

nickels to her budget, she also painted greeting cards at night after Harry went to sleep, especially fancy Valentines. Her heartache, however, was not yet over—Robert did not return from the war.

For many years, Lois believed that she was a war widow, but the truth was just as cruel. Robert had done quite well in the military; he had attained the rank of major, a commission that was signed personally by President Lincoln. He had served with distinction alongside General Pope and General Granger. In February 1865, he was honorably discharged and returned to civilian life, but not to his wife and remaining child. It wasn't until 1873 that Lois received word that Robert had been killed in a railroad accident. Some sources claim that he died in Minnesota and others Missouri. Based on his Civil War assignments, Missouri seems the most likely location. In any case, it must have been a horrible shock to Lois; the husband whom she thought she had lost a decade earlier in battle had actually deserted her and their child. Throughout his life, Harry claimed that his father had died in the war; the truth was probably too painful. In some ways, though, he was correct—Robert had essentially been dead to the family since his failure to return.

126   JACKSON DIRECTORY.

THE OLD MAMMOTH!

Camp, Winters & Co

𝔍𝔪𝔭𝔬𝔯𝔱𝔢𝔯𝔰, 𝔍𝔬𝔟𝔟𝔢𝔯𝔰

AND

Retailers of

DRY GOODS,

ETC.,

NO. 270 MAIN STREET,

JACKSON, MICH.

H. W. CAMP.   A. L. WINTERS.   W. M. BENNETT.

BOSTWICK & GOULD, Attorneys and Real Estate Agts.

An 1867 advertisement for Camp, Winters & Company. Harry Selfridge began working for this dry goods firm when he was just ten years old. Within the year, the store took on a new partner and was renamed Camp, Morrill & Camp.

Although Lois struggled to provide for her son, she never gave up hope for a brighter future and didn't let Harry dwell on their meager circumstances. She immersed herself in uplifting and inspirational literature, collecting "Great Thoughts" as some women collected dolls or thimbles. She instilled in Harry impeccable manners and a habit of meticulous grooming. Most importantly, she encouraged him to think big; it was a trait that served him well. In his later years, Harry told *American Magazine* about a little game that he and his mother would play almost every evening. They called it "Supposing," and it made the child's imagination soar. They might not have had enough money for toys or other diversions, but Lois ensured that her surviving son knew how to dream about life's possibilities. He recounted:

[M]*other would say something like this, "suppose when you grow older and have a little position and are making a tiny salary, you come home some night and say, 'Mother, they have advanced my pay a dollar a week. Now we shall be able to save something.'…a year or two after that you come home and say 'Mother, I have saved enough money now to start in business for myself'…a year or two more passes, and then one night you might come home and say, 'Mother, I have a surprise for you…I have bought a house.*

*We are going to have our own little cottage with a bay window…' And then
you come home and say, 'Mother, I have another surprise for you…' and
you take me outside and show me a horse and buggy."*

Although the game might have varied, the underlying message did not:
anything was possible for the person who was industrious and clever and
refused to quit. But even Lois likely could not have dreamed of the grandiose
future that the simple game foretold.

From an early age, Harry was fascinated with money—or, more correctly, the
earning of it. As a child, he delivered newspapers for the *Citizen Patriot* and
jumped at any odd job that he could perform for a few extra pennies. At the
age of ten, while his peers enjoyed lazy summer pastimes such as baseball
and fishing during the school break, he found full-time employment, earning
$1.50 per week sweeping floors and performing other chores at a dry goods
store named Camp, Winters & Company—later Camp, Morrill & Camp—in
downtown Jackson. The establishment adjoined another dry goods and rug
business owned by a gentleman named Leonard Field, whose cousin Marshall
was making quite a name for himself in fast-growing Chicago. Harry worked
feverishly at the job, often working ten-hour days. His enthusiasm and aptitude
did not go unnoticed; soon he was entrusted with stocking and arranging
merchandise and, later, with account collections. Of course, he dutifully
handed his weekly salary over to Lois to help with household expenses. As the
new school year approached at summer's end, he begged his mother to allow
him to continue working instead of returning to his lessons. Lois would have
none of it, though, and insisted that he proceed with his education. Eventually
they compromised: Harry would return to school but would spend most of his
evenings and weekends at the store.

By the time he reached his thirteenth birthday, Harry was developing
some of the entrepreneurial and promotional skills that defined him later in
life. He and a schoolmate, Peter "Burr" Loomis, had created a monthly boys'
magazine named *Will o' the Wisp*. It was not a simple childhood lark; Harry
methodically called on each local business, selling advertising on the promise
of guaranteed distribution to all the boys at his school. And if the advertiser
couldn't pay in cash, he wasn't opposed to bartering. When one dentist didn't
settle his account promptly, Harry negotiated some free dental work instead.
The experience instilled in him both a love of writing and a deep respect
for the power of advertising. In later years, when Selfridge's of London was
well known, he delighted in writing a series of essays on business, philosophy

and general topics under the pen name of "Callisthenes." Named after Callisthenes of Olynthus, a Greek historian and great-nephew of Aristotle, these columns appeared daily in dozens of newspapers for a period of nearly thirty years. Actually, they were thinly veiled advertisements for the store, and Selfridge had to pay to publish them. The earliest versions began with a note that read, "This Column is occupied every day by an article reflecting the policies, principles, and opinions of this House of Business upon various points of public interest." They were simply signed "Selfridge & Co., Ltd." Sometimes they contained the initials of the contributor, but in most cases they were either written—or heavily edited—by Selfridge himself. It was an obscure yet successful way of keeping the great store's name in the public consciousness, but it wasn't inexpensive. An associate once estimated that Selfridge spent more than £60,000 over the years to place the essays—approximately $2 million in today's money.

Harry's experience with *Will o' the Wisp* also proved valuable in an unexpected way: Burr Loomis's father, P.B. Loomis, owned a small bank on Main Street in Jackson. He was impressed with Harry's intelligence and hard work, and so he offered the boy a full-time job as a junior clerk. Harry was just fourteen years old, but the starting salary of twenty dollars per month would go a long way toward putting groceries on the table. Lois had since been promoted to headmistress of Jackson High School, but money was still very tight. She pleaded with Harry to remain in school, but he was adamant this time—he wanted to begin his career. But he wouldn't be satisfied with his junior position for long. He wanted to keep the books, and he pestered Mr. Potter, the bank's head teller and accountant, for the opportunity. Potter was a cantankerous sort and had little faith that the pushy young lad could handle such responsibility. Selfridge, however, proposed a deal: he would post the books for one month under Potter's watchful eye. If, at the end of the month, there were no errors or "blots," Harry would be allowed to continue the tasks. Not surprisingly, his work was flawless, and by the time he reached his sixteenth birthday, he was the head clerk and earning a salary of thirty dollars per month. In his later years, he often mentioned with some pride that he had trained in a bank.

Of course, it wasn't long before broader horizons beckoned. Most sources claim that at about this time, Harry applied for acceptance into the U.S. Naval Academy in Annapolis, Maryland. It certainly wouldn't be hard to imagine—the extended Selfridge family had spawned three navy admirals and later an army first lieutenant who gained a tragic notoriety in his own right. Robert Etholen Selfridge was assigned to the Aeronautical Division,

U.S. Signal Corps at Fort Myers, Virginia, as one of the nation's first military pilots. On September 17, 1908, Orville Wright traveled to the base to demonstrate the Wright Flyer for possible military use. With Lieutenant Selfridge on board as a passenger and observer, Wright slowly circled the field at a height of about 150 feet. After several passes, disaster struck when a propeller blade broke loose and tore into the rudder controls. The aircraft was thrown into a steep dive, and it crashed into the ground nose first. Wright was later quoted as saying, "Our course for 50 feet was within a very few degrees of the perpendicular." Both men were severely injured. Wright spent seven weeks in the hospital with multiple fractures, and Selfridge died from a traumatic brain injury just three hours after the crash, becoming America's first military casualty of powered flight.

Harry, however, was not destined for a distinguished military career like his distant cousins. For reasons that are still obscure, he was denied entrance to Annapolis. Harry always claimed that his height—variously reported as between five feet, five and a half inches, and five feet, eight and a half inches—fell half an inch below entrance requirements. In truth, he would not have been denied for that reason, as the academy's regulations only required that a candidate be "not less than five feet" in stature. Given his intelligence, it's also highly unlikely that he failed on academic grounds. There are many other possibilities, such as eyesight; Harry was rather far-sighted and was dependent on his thick spectacles. He might also have been turned away due to his weight and build. Unlike the modern-day military that would seek to exclude obese recruits, early militias were much more concerned about underweight candidates who might be harboring tuberculosis or other communicable wasting diseases. The Naval Academy exam included chest circumference in an effort to weed out the frail. Harry was always referred to as "compact," even "diminutive," so perhaps that worked against him. Yet another interesting twist was uncovered by author Gordon Honeycombe after he researched this issue in honor of Selfridge's seventy-fifth anniversary. Honeycombe claimed that the academy showed no record of Harry's application, although it maintained archives of even the unsuccessful candidates. It's quite possible that the whole story was simply fabricated by Selfridge in an attempt to add color to the narrative of his childhood history.

In any case, Harry quickly moved on. Bored with the bank and presumably turned away by the military, he found a position as head bookkeeper for a furniture factory in Jackson named Gilbert, Ransom & Knapp. Here he was earning a rather respectable salary of fifty dollars per month and

196   JACKSON DIRECTORY.

GILBERT, RANSOM & KNAPP,

(SUCCESSORS TO HENRY GILBERT,)

Manufacturers & Dealers in

CABINET FURNITURE

IN ROSEWOOD, MAHOGANY & WALNUT,

SPRING BEDS, MATTRESSES & LOUNGES

WILLOW-WARE,

Picture Frames,

Mouldings, Mirrors, &c.,

Jackson, ▪ Michigan.

Manufactory at the Michigan State Prison. Warehouse
and Salesroom, No. 258 Main Street.

HENRY GILBERT,	D. SEYMOUR GILBERT.
EDWIN A. CARDER,	HENRY C. RANSOM,
JOHN McKEE.	HOLLIS F. KNAPP

Farms, City Lots, Dwellings and Wild Lands for Sale by

Selfridge worked briefly as a bookkeeper at Gilbert, Ransom & Knapp, a Jackson furniture manufacturer. Although he was quite content in the position, the firm became insolvent and closed its doors.

seemed quite content. Unfortunately, it didn't last for long. The factory was overextended and undercapitalized, and the country was poised to enter a severe financial depression that began in 1873 when Jay Cooke and Company, one of the strongest financial institutions in the United States, suddenly closed its doors after being squeezed by inflation and speculation. The closing set off a panic that caused stocks to tumble and numerous banks to fail. Harry's bosses were forced to liquidate, and he was suddenly unemployed. Jobs were scarce in the face of the downturn, and Jackson didn't offer much in the way of opportunities. So, Selfridge reluctantly left behind his hometown for a position at an insurance agency in Big Rapids, a rural community roughly 160 miles to the northwest. The pay was only about half of what he had been earning, and the small town didn't offer much in the way of amusements, especially for the relatively "citified" Selfridge. While acquaintances hunted and fished, Harry read books and played poker. It would also be one of the few times in his life that he was separated from his mother for any significant duration. It was likely a very lonely time for the young man.

Harry, however, was not one to overlook any opportunity. He used his spare time to begin a correspondence course in law. Perhaps he would become an esteemed trial lawyer and provide Lois with that cottage and horse and buggy she so coveted. But the attempt was, in Harry's words, a "complete and utter disaster." He apparently had no aptitude for the law, and he found the studies tiresome and draining. After about three years in Big Rapids, he quit his job at the agency and returned to Jackson. He had $500 in his pocket and no plans for the future. Although he claimed to have saved the money through careful budgeting, some biographers suspect that the cache had been greatly enhanced by his skills at poker. Indeed, gambling would remain a cherished pastime throughout his life, and one that would contribute greatly to his eventual decline.

Once back in Jackson, Selfridge accepted a job as a clerk at a grocery shop named Palmer and Selover. He toyed with the idea of buying into the firm as a partner, but he soon realized that there simply wasn't that much room for growth and expansion. He desperately wanted to be a merchant, but his dreams were much more expansive than the relatively humble business opportunities that Jackson had to offer. By now, he had reached his twenties,

A delivery wagon for the L.H. Field Company, whose business adjoined Camp, Winters & Company. Leonard Field was also a casual friend of Lois Selfridge's.

and he found himself bored, frustrated and still not very far from the painful clutches of poverty that he had endured as a child. He wanted to show his mother that he was worthy of her faith in him and that he could make all those "supposings" come true. He later told an associate that he had experienced an epiphany around this time: "I realized it was not so much the immediate position and salary that mattered as where a position would eventually lead."

While Harry pondered this new wisdom, an old acquaintance reentered his life—Leonard Field, the neighboring merchant from his days at Camp, Morrill & Camp. Field was a casual friend of Lois Selfridge, and it's quite possible that Lois reached out to him for advice and direction. In any case, he had an intriguing proposal: would Harry like to travel to Chicago to work for Leonard's cousin Marshall? It was 1879, and the dry goods emporium of Field, Leiter and Company was redefining Chicago retail. In addition, the firm had a booming wholesale business and foreign buying offices across Europe. It was a surprisingly tough decision for Selfridge. On one hand, it was quite obvious that the potential for growth in Chicago was nearly unlimited. On the other hand, Harry had just been offered a job as head bookkeeper at a local dairy for the astounding salary of $1,200 per year, enough to allow him to join the ranks of Jackson's well-heeled upper class. Should he take the safe and sure route or risk it all and move away to the big city? In the end, Lois convinced him to take the long view. She quoted Robert Louis Stevenson: "To travel hopefully is a better thing than to arrive." The decision was made: Harry would depart for Chicago with a letter of introduction from Leonard Field tucked in his breast pocket. He was twenty-three years old and about to enter a world unlike any he had ever experienced. But he was determined to thrive.

MR. FIELD'S STOCK BOY

I am an adventurer.
—Harry Gordon Selfridge

The Chicago that greeted Selfridge when he stepped off the train in 1879 was a bustling young metropolis that was growing at a phenomenal rate. Just fifty years earlier, it had been a remote fur trading post situated at the mouth of a swampy river, with only about thirty permanent residents. By the time Harry arrived, more than half a million people called the city home, and it had grown to be the country's third-largest manufacturing center, surpassed only by New York and Philadelphia. To understand the transformation, it's necessary to regress a bit.

Chicago had, quite literally, risen from the mud. In its early days, even the slightest rainfall turned the narrow unpaved streets back into the bog they had once been. William Butler Ogden, the son of a New York real estate and lumber tycoon, came to Chicago in the 1830s to inspect some land purchased sight-unseen by his brother-in-law. After sinking past his ankles into the oozing earth, he wrote back home, "You've been victim of the worst kind of folly." Ogden stayed anyway and soon became Chicago's first mayor, but mud and sanitation issues continued to plague the populace until deadly cholera outbreaks in 1849 and 1854 forced the city fathers to come up with a plan. They turned to an engineer named Ellis Sylvester Chesbrough, who had successfully designed a water distribution system for Boston.

A young Harry Gordon Selfridge. This photo
dates from Harry's early years in Chicago.

It was obvious that Chicago needed a sewer and drainage system, but those methods were always based on gravity. Because the city's land was at almost the same elevation as Lake Michigan and the Chicago River, gravity drainage wouldn't work. After some study, Chesbrough came up with the only workable solution: they must raise the city. And in a spectacular feat of engineering, they did just that. Workers dug under buildings and placed jackscrews beneath the foundations. Once in place, hundreds of laborers would simultaneously turn the screws, raising the building into the air, sometimes ten feet or more. Once this was accomplished, sewer pipes were laid underneath and covered with mud dredged from the river. Finally, a new foundation would be built. In one instance, an entire city block of four- and five-story brick buildings was raised in a single operation. Curious pedestrians wandered underneath, marveling at the buildings that now seemed to be suspended in midair. Eventually, the street grade would be built up as well. Amazingly, buildings did not close during the process but rather continued business as usual. One confused guest at the Tremont Hotel couldn't understand why the stairs leading from the street to the lobby became steeper during his stay or why the once street-level windows were now over his head.

As the city grew, so did its mercantile trade. Retailers and wholesalers alike flocked to the area to take advantage of the exploding population growth. One of the most successful was a young New Yorker named Potter Palmer. The feminist movement was increasing in popularity as women began to demand equal rights, and Palmer knew that as women gained more independence, they would soon become a significant economic force. The dark and crowded dry goods stores of the day held little appeal for female shoppers. Some even doubled as taverns, and a proper lady would scurry in to complete a necessary purchase and leave as quickly as possible. Browsing was highly discouraged, and all sales were final.

Potter changed all that. His store on Lake Street was airy and bright, and the merchandise was displayed in an attractive manner. He carried everything from rough calicos to expensive Paris silks, and each customer, rich or poor, was treated with the same unerring courtesy. Ladies were encouraged to touch and examine the goods and could even bring items home for their husband's opinion. If the purchase was deemed unsatisfactory, it could be returned for a full refund. Other merchants laughed derisively at what they considered

The Field, Leiter and Company store on Chicago's State Street, circa 1871.

Potter's foolishness. His instincts were correct, however, and soon P. Palmer & Company was one of the premier retail establishments in town. But Potter knew that eventually he would have to slow down. He was only thirty-eight years old, but his hard-driven lifestyle had already begun to affect his health; his doctor insisted that he scale back the breakneck pace. He was already a millionaire many times over and had substantial real estate holdings in the city. It would soon come time for him to sell his dry goods business. However, he didn't want to hand it over to just anyone—he hoped to find a buyer who would maintain the high level of service and integrity on which he had built the business. Luckily, it wouldn't take him long to find the right candidate, and it would be a young Yankee trader very much like him.

Marshall Field, the son of a farmer in Conway, Massachusetts, had arrived in Chicago just eight years earlier. He knew from an early age that he wanted to be a merchant and quickly found employment at one of Palmer's competitors, Cooley, Farwell & Company. The firm was primarily a wholesaler, but it did have a small retail operation where Marshall began as a clerk. Like Palmer, Field had an intuitive understanding of what female shoppers were seeking. He waited on them with rapt attention, listening to every word they spoke and patiently answering all their questions. It wasn't long before even the wealthiest and most demanding customers were requesting to see the young Mr. Field rather than one of the experienced, longtime salesmen who had served them previously. The owners of the company were suitably impressed and quickly promoted Marshall to a position in wholesale sales. He spent the next several years traveling from one remote prairie town to the next, showing his samples and writing up orders. In the past, small-town proprietors had to make an arduous trek by horse and wagon to the nearest large city to purchase stock for their stores. They were limited to whatever inventory was on hand or whatever they could fit into their wagon. That had all changed with the coming of the railroads. Now they could study an illustrated catalogue at their leisure—or even view samples when the salesman rode into town—and their orders would be delivered to the nearest depot. They could order a wider variety of products and place orders more frequently. The wholesale business was booming.

But in 1857, a financial crisis struck. It began with the failure of Ohio Life Insurance and Trust Company and quickly spread to a nationwide run on banks as investors withdrew their funds. More than five thousand businesses failed in one year, including railroads and banks. Grain prices tumbled, leading to severe hardship in the agricultural core of the United States. The panic spread to Europe, the Far East and South America in what was probably the first example of the developing global economy. Stock prices dropped precipitously, and as unemployment rose, riots broke out in some cities. Chicago had been growing so quickly and was so prosperous that it was spared the worst of the crisis, but its economy did suffer. Many of Cooley & Farwell's competitors closed up, and "Ceasing Business" and "Distress Sale" signs peppered the retail district. Only one merchant seemed largely unaffected by the crunch, and that was Potter Palmer. He did temporarily discontinue his small wholesale business, but he actually expanded his retail during this time and moved to larger quarters. Palmer purchased goods at rock-bottom prices from panicked wholesalers on the East Coast and then passed those savings along to his customers, offering fresh inventory at reasonable prices.

None of this was lost on Field. He had taken careful note of each competitor's strategy, and he analyzed what had worked and what hadn't. It was obvious to him that Palmer's ideas had worked. Soon the economy rebounded, and Marshall was made a junior partner at Cooley & Farwell, while Cooley moved to New York to handle purchasing. Palmer also opened a New York buying office around this time and began to send buyers to Europe. Palmer had realized that by cutting out the middleman importers, he could buy and ultimately sell at prices lower than his competitors. Once again, Field watched with great interest.

For a few years, it was business as usual, until another economic crisis

Marshall Field, in a photo taken shortly before his death in 1906.

struck: the beginning of the Civil War in 1861. Due to general fears and the uncertainty of trade, especially the availability of Southern cotton, a rapidly escalating period of inflation hit the country. The value of the dollar plummeted, and the price of goods skyrocketed. Most merchants cut back on purchases, fearing an inevitable collapse and deflation, but Palmer, who had since resumed wholesale trade, continued to buy large amounts of inventory at the highly inflated rates. Competitors shook their heads in bewilderment, but as usual, his gamble paid off. By the time the war was winding down, prices had nearly doubled and goods were scarce. While his rivals struggled to restock, Palmer had warehouses filled with desirable inventory that was now worth significantly more than he had paid. He could beat everyone on price and selection. His instincts seemed flawless.

Eventually, Cooley retired, Field became a senior partner and the new firm of Farwell, Field & Company was born. The men took on a junior partner, Levi Leiter, who had been the firm's lead accountant for many years. While Farwell and Leiter stayed in Chicago, Field moved to New York to take on the buying that Cooley had done. Field, no doubt taking his lead from Palmer's example, began an aggressive buying campaign, filling warehouses and stockrooms to their limits. Within months, the *Chicago Tribune* named Farwell & Field the top wholesale house in the city. But although they were quite successful, none of the partners was particularly happy. Field wanted to expand the business greatly, while Farwell was content for things to remain the same. Their very different personalities and goals created constant friction. Field was frustrated and began casting about for a fresh opportunity. Levi also wanted to leave and join forces with Field, but the two of them together only had access to a combined capital of a little more than $300,000, not nearly enough cash to build a competitive firm from scratch.

What Field didn't know is that while he had been watching Potter Palmer and studying his methods, Palmer had also been watching him with a great deal of respect. Actually, the two were very much alike; both were ethical, honest, hardworking, creative and committed to providing the best service and goods to their customers. When Palmer heard that Field and Leiter were considering leaving their partnership with Farwell, he knew that the time had come to follow his doctor's advice to slow down—he had finally found the right successors. In late 1864, he approached the men with an offer almost too good to be true: he would sell them his entire business for 20 percent below the inventory value, provided they accept his brother, Milton, as a junior partner. But Potter was no fool; he realized that the money Field and Leiter possessed would not be sufficient to capitalize the firm, so he agreed to remain a silent partner and leave $330,000 in the business until such time as they could afford to buy him out. Field put in $250,000, and Leiter scraped together $120,000. Milton would also contribute $50,000, bringing the total capitalized value to $750,000. The new firm was named Field, Palmer and Leiter, with the "Palmer" referring to Milton, not Potter. The new business thrived, and within two years, Field and Leiter were able to buy out the Potter brothers.

Finally divested of his dry goods business, Palmer sailed off to Europe for an extended vacation. He planned to stay away for three years, but in less than a year he was back and once again hard at work. This time he turned his attention to real estate. He knew that Lake Street, which was then Chicago's "street of merchants," could not continue to anchor a sustainable business district. It was hemmed in between the river and railroad tracks and was off the path of the streetcar lines. There was no room for growth. Even worse, its proximity to the river, which was virtually an open sewer at the time, made shopping unbearable for much of the year. The stench of human waste and rotting animal carcasses permeated the air, causing shoppers to hurry from store to store with handkerchiefs pressed tightly against their noses lest they retch and gag at the odors. Palmer had a vision of a brand-new shopping district away from the river, with plenty of room to grow and easy access to transportation, and he decided that State Street would be the location.

Once again, his detractors laughed and questioned his sanity. State Street was then a narrow and rutted country lane, peppered with dusty saloons, bordellos and run-down shacks. His plan seemed crazy and doomed to fail. Palmer paid the critics no mind, however, and set about work. He purchased almost all the frontage on State for nearly a mile and tore down or moved back the existing buildings to create a wide boulevard. On the north end, at the corner of Washington and State, he built a limestone and marble building that towered six stories above the street, with a façade of dramatic white Corinthian columns reaching toward the sky. It was the most beautiful building in the city, and all it needed was the right tenant. And he knew that tenant should be none other than Field, Leiter and Company. The partners were hesitant at first—Palmer was asking an astronomical $50,000 per year for rent—but Field trusted Palmer's instincts. So, in late 1868, they moved from their cramped quarters on Lake Street and into the gleaming marble palace on State. The other merchants on Lake, who had scoffed disdainfully at "Potter's folly," watched sheepishly as customers flocked to the new store in such numbers that the newspapers heralded the store's opening as a newsworthy event. One by one, they quietly packed up their stock and followed Field to State.

But Palmer wasn't finished. On the south end of his holdings, he built a fabulous eight-story hotel of granite and Italian marble named, of course, the Palmer House, as a gift to his new bride, Bertha Honore. The two had been introduced by Marshall Field, and Palmer was madly in love with the young debutante. She was twenty-three years his junior, but she stepped easily into her role as queen of Chicago's social set. He spent $200,000 to build the hotel as a tribute and another $100,000 to fill it with luxurious decorations. Tragically, it would burn to the ground in the Great Chicago Fire just thirteen days after opening in 1871. Palmer, undeterred, immediately started construction on a new and even more spectacular building, this time built of brick and iron, and later advertised it as the "World's Only Fireproof Hotel."

Of course, when the Great Fire struck, it burned a full third of the city, including Field and Leiter's grand store and most of the commercial district. But as Chicago began to rebuild, Palmer decided to sell the Washington and State corner property to the fast-growing Singer Sewing Machine Company in order to raise capital for his new hotel. The Singer Company quickly began to construct another elaborate retail palace on the site, while Field and Leiter made the best of their temporary relocation to a refurbished horse barn. Once the new building was complete, they resumed business on State Street, but in a cruel bit of déjà vu, it burned to the ground in yet another fire in 1877. The *Chicago Tribune* eulogized it in an editorial: "The destruction of St. Peter's in Rome could hardly have aroused a deeper interest than the destruction of this splendid dry goods establishment…this was the place of worship for thousands of our female fellow-citizens. It was the only shrine at which they paid their devotions." An exaggeration perhaps, but it did sum up the great fondness that Chicagoans had for their iconic hometown store. Once again the Singer folks rebuilt, even grander this time, and in 1879, Field and Leiter negotiated a purchase instead of renting. It was this splendid new building that Selfridge stepped into when he arrived for his interview with Marshall Field.

Selfridge later bragged that he "sold" himself to Field, but it's likely that Field would have hired him anyway as a favor to his cousin Leonard. In describing the interview, Harry claimed that it lasted just a few minutes and that Field was so cold it "made him shiver." In reality, Field was never known as a particularly cold or stern man, but he did prefer to listen rather than speak—so much so that he had gained the nickname of "Silent Marsh." In spite of this possibly intimidating quirk, most of his employees considered him an exceptionally caring and fair man. In one instance that occurred after Selfridge's hiring, a young errand boy was caught stealing money from a customer's purse. When confronted, he tearfully explained that his parents were both ill and had no money to see a doctor, and the household had very little food. That evening, in a kind gesture, Selfridge quietly made his way to the family's run-down tenement with a basket of food. On his way up the dark staircase, he met one of Field's drivers coming down. Field had felt the same pangs of sympathy and had sent over a large box of food and other provisions,

Harry Gordon Selfridge during his twenties, about the time he arrived in Chicago.

apparently including some funds for a doctor. Harry later told a friend, "That's the kind of man he was."

Although Harry loved retail, that wasn't where he started with Field and Leiter. In fact, he didn't even start at the awe-inspiring State Street store. His first position was as a lowly stock boy in the wholesale department's basement storeroom at Market and Madison Streets. He later claimed that his salary was ten dollars per week, but even that might have been an exaggeration. In any case, he was likely earning less than he had earned as a bookkeeper at age seventeen. But Harry knew that Lois was right. What better way to make a fortune than to learn from the undisputed king of Chicago merchants? He worked hard, saved judiciously and sent a portion of his weekly earnings back home to his mother in Jackson. It wouldn't take long for someone with his skills and drive to move ahead.

At the time, the head of the wholesale division was a man by the name of John Graves Shedd. Like Field, Shedd was a New England farm boy who had come west to make his fortune. And like Selfridge, he had started

John G. Shedd was both a rival and friend of Selfridge's during his years at Marshall Field's.

with Field as a stock boy. He had moved up the ladder quite rapidly and was a fine example of Field's predilection for cultivating talent from within the organization. Shedd and Selfridge got along well and shared a mutual respect. Harry's son, Gordon Jr., later wrote that "Shedd was probably father's greatest personal friend, with, to my knowledge, nothing to break the friendship from first to last." Harry had worked in the stockroom for less than a year when Shedd promoted him to a traveling sales position. Selfridge would be responsible for the entire state of Illinois, carrying his samples of linen and lace to the distant small towns that dotted the vast prairie. There's no record of how he performed at the job, and Harry rarely spoke about it, but apparently he hated it. He wanted to be in the city, not traveling from one monotonous rural outpost to another. After three years, he approached Field and asked for a transfer to retail.

Much had changed in the few years since Harry had come to Chicago. Probably the most significant was the dissolution of the partnership between Marshall Field and Levi Leiter. Although the two had built a very prosperous business together, they were polar opposites in personality. Leiter had a volatile temper and had become increasingly irascible and distrustful over the years. He had once chased away a wholesale customer—

calling him a sneak and a thief—solely because the man sported gray hair and a black moustache. In Leiter's mind, the likelihood that the man had dyed his facial hair indicated some sort of dishonesty and weak moral character. He also hated retail and fought any attempt to expand. By 1881, Field had run out of patience. The partnership agreement between the principals was expiring, and Field had no intention of renewing it. He offered two options: he would buy out Leiter, or Leiter could make him an offer. There was really no choice to be made. Leiter knew that he had none of the skills that made Field successful, and he had always remained in the background, concentrating primarily on keeping the books. He was also a very rich man at that point, with extensive real estate holdings, and didn't really need to work any longer. And so, in January 1881, Leiter quietly announced his "retirement" from the firm, telling reporters that he was going to go trout fishing. Effective immediately, the firm's name would be Marshall Field & Company. That same year, Harry had brought Lois to Chicago and set her up in a lovely apartment just off of Lake Shore Drive. They would never be far apart again.

Field did agree to Selfridge's transfer to retail, but with one stipulation: there was no turning back. "You have made your choice," said Field. "Go to retail. But there you stay. Your future with us is there, and nowhere else. Do you understand?" Harry did indeed understand, and he couldn't have been happier. He had recently taken a vacation to the East Coast, where he visited the finest retail stores in New York, Philadelphia and Boston. The trip had greatly excited him and filled his head with lofty ideas that he longed to implement. Unfortunately, in his new position, he would be reporting to the longstanding head of the retail division, a crusty old gent named J.M. Fleming. Fleming was, to put it politely, set in his ways. He had no intention of allowing this brash newcomer—a mere junior clerk at that—to make any changes to the status quo. They locked horns from the very start. Often, their arguments would spill over into Field's office. Field was not a micromanager and would usually tell his department heads to use their own best judgment. In these disputes, however, he would always listen carefully to both sides. While he probably agreed with Fleming's assessment that Selfridge was impetuous and pushy, Field was a visionary and could recognize the merit in many of Harry's ideas. Invariably, he would gently coax Fleming to give it a try and "see if it makes us money." It almost always did.

Within a year, Harry was promoted to assistant manager of retail at nearly double his salary. Oddly enough, in later years his son, Gordon Jr., would claim that Harry had never worked directly in retail but had instead served in an advertising and promotional position. Although there's no doubt that Selfridge produced most of the store's advertising copy during this time, he was indeed working the sales floor; it appears that Gordon Jr. was simply misled by one of his father's revisionist recollections. In any case, now that he had earned Field's trust and support, Harry began to implement some of those ideas that had swirled in his imagination. The retail business flourished, and Fleming had little ammunition to argue against the changes. Eventually, Selfridge was given Fleming's job—retail general manager—at a salary of $5,000 per year. After many years of struggling and supposing, his career, it seemed, was finally on the proper trajectory.

SELFRIDGE'S INFLUENCE

Develop imagination—throw away the routine.
—Harry Gordon Selfridge

Harry Gordon Selfridge was a brilliant yet quirky man who had an astounding ability to discern the needs and motivations of shoppers, and yet he was seemingly blind to the compulsions and demons that drove him to his eventual downfall. He demanded nothing short of complete honesty in his dealings with customers; all goods had to be exactly as they were represented. "We allow no misstatements" was his motto. And yet he embellished and falsified so much about his own life that even close friends and relatives were at a loss to pin down any absolute truth. And although he was extremely intelligent and well read, he held fast to certain odd superstitions. He was greatly suspicious of tall men and believed that men with thin necks lacked courage and energy. He once explained to a colleague that thin-necked men didn't have proper blood flow to their brains and therefore couldn't sustain deep thought without becoming confused and fatigued. His belief in these theories was so strong that it dictated his hiring practices. A tall man with a slender neck didn't have much chance of being hired by Selfridge, no matter what his qualifications were.

Appearances meant everything to Selfridge. He was always meticulously groomed and dressed in the finest fashion. Each morning, at precisely 8:00 a.m., a barber arrived at his office to shave him and trim and wax his moustache and eyebrows. Afterward, Harry would dress in one of the dozen or more crisply pressed suits with silk lapels he kept tucked away in his office wardrobe. His assortment of custom-made linen shirts with high wing collars—designed especially to accommodate his thick neck—were always perfectly starched, and the row of gleaming black patent shoes had nary a smudge. He was known to change his suit and shirt at least once a day, sometimes more. The gold-rimmed pince-nez that he required for reading dangled from a thick gold chain, and he was never without a flower in his lapel. As his position grew, he favored exotic orchids over the relatively pedestrian rose boutonnière.

His words tumbled out rapidly, his voice high-pitched and usually breathless. Harry always carried himself in an erect and regal manner, but he rushed about as if late for a train. It was no wonder that he quickly acquired the nickname "Mile-a-Minute Harry." It also explains why he and "Silent Marsh" sometimes had difficulty communicating. His detractors called him effeminate, self-absorbed and conceited, although most women found him quite attractive. But he paid little attention to the ladies during his early years with Field's. His only companion in the evenings was his mother, with whom he often visited the theater or the symphony. The store was his mistress and his all-consuming passion.

Once Harry assumed the position of retail general manager and was free of Fleming's shackles, he immediately began to make the changes he had before only dreamed about. Field had always kept up to date with the technology of the day, but Selfridge believed that it could be improved. The store was one of the first in the city to boast electric lights, which were powered internally by a seventy-five-horsepower engine and two dynamos rigged up in the subbasement, but Selfridge insisted on quadrupling the number of fixtures so that every corner of the interior was brightly lit and cheery. He placed electric lighting in the expansive windows so that the attractive displays were illuminated at night for pedestrians who might want to window-shop. Field had already installed telephones in key areas, but Selfridge wanted to speed up communications. He installed a switchboard operated by a pleasant and well-trained young woman and wired extensions to every key department.

Next, Harry turned his attention to the merchandising fixtures. Dry goods stores of the day typically featured high shelves behind a tall counter lined with stools. A customer would sit while an associate pulled out samples to view. Selfridge recognized that this approach prevented the shopper from truly engaging with the goods and certainly discouraged impulse purchases. He dragged tables laden with merchandise out into the aisles so that people

The women's waiting room at Marshall Field's offered comfy leather couches, private writing desks and spacious tables for ladies who wished to rest or socialize during a long day of shopping.

could pick up and examine items without relying on a commission-hungry associate. The approach encouraged customers to browse and greatly increased sales. The back shelves and the counter were also lowered so that goods were more accessible and could be displayed near eye level.

Up to this point, Field was agreeable to the changes and pleased with the results. But he and Harry were certainly at odds about the next idea: Selfridge wanted to put a restaurant in the store. "This is a dry goods store. We don't feed people here!" thundered Field. Harry reasoned that serving food would keep the customers in the store longer and create more opportunity for sales. Marshall was unconvinced but finally agreed to give it a try. There's an apocryphal tale often told that claims to explain how the first tearoom came to be. The story says that in early 1890, a millinery clerk named Mrs. Sarah Hering was assisting some ladies in her department. Just when it seemed like they were ready to make a purchase, one woman complained of feeling weak because she had not eaten all day. An unescorted woman of that era would not dream of stepping into one of the rowdy pubs along the street, so she would have to return home for a meal. Perhaps out of concern for the customer, or perhaps unwilling to lose a large sale, Mrs. Hering pulled out a small table and chairs and offered the women the lunch she had prepared for herself, a chicken potpie. They were delighted and asked if she would

Marshall Field's Tea Room offered tired shoppers a delightful spot to relax and enjoy a delicious meal.

allow them to return the next day with some of their wealthy friends. Mrs. Hering agreed, and the following afternoon, armed with potpies she had baked at home, she placed tables in the back of her department and hosted an impromptu luncheon. Although it's a charming tale, it's an unlikely one. But there really was a Mrs. Hering who worked in the store at that time, and her recipe for chicken potpie became such a popular menu item that it's still the featured dish in the former Marshall Field's Walnut Room.

In truth, the restaurant was carefully planned and designed once Selfridge received Field's reluctant approval. Named simply the "Tea Room," it opened in April 1890 on the third floor, near the fur department. On the first day, fifty-six curious shoppers lunched on a menu that included Mrs. Hering's chicken potpie, corned beef hash, chicken salad, orange punch served in an orange shell and an ice cream concoction named Marshall Field's Rose Punch. There were fifteen tables attended by eight waitresses and four cooks. In Selfridge's typical grand and dramatic style, each place setting showcased a single long-stemmed red rose resting on the plate. Talk of Field's latest feature—arguably the first restaurant in a department store—was all over town, and within the year, the Tea Room was serving 1,500 meals per day. Apparently even Selfridge was amazed at the response, and other restaurants

The elegant Narcissus Room restaurant was named for the sculpture of the Greek god Narcissus that graces the beautiful central fountain.

quickly followed. In fact, within a few years Marshall Field's boasted a total of seven in-store eateries, including the Circassian-paneled Walnut Room, the Narcissus Room and the Men's Grill with its Tiffany fountain and plush leather chairs.

Selfridge believed that a department store should be more than just a temple of commerce. He envisioned a place where people could go for various services, where they could meet friends, have a meal or simply relax. Field had already started down that path by offering amenities such as a reading and writing room, a ladies' lounge, a silent room for resting and a medical bureau, but there was plenty more to come. The store soon boasted dozens of specialty departments, including an optician's bench where a customer could be fitted for a new pair of eyeglasses or have an old pair repaired; a glove cleaning service; fur cleaning and storage, so that a wealthy lady needn't clutter her wardrobe during the summer months; jewelry and shoe repair; a photographic department that sold cameras and developed film plates; and custom tailoring and upholstery services. Between 1883 and 1904, Field's tripled the number of departments from 50 to 150. The limited concept of a dry goods store no longer applied. Field and Selfridge, and a handful of their merchant peers, had created an entirely new shopping experience: the American department store.

Selfridge was now confident that he could entice customers to linger and shop once they entered the premises. His next goal was to draw more people through the doors. Marshall Field & Company already enjoyed the loyalty—and the dollars—of most of Chicago's elite, but there was little inventory that could accommodate the budget of the hordes of poor immigrants who made up the backbone of the city's labor force. After mulling it over, Harry came up with an ingenious if somewhat risky plan. It made no sense to bring in a selection of inexpensive merchandise to draw in the less fortunate; that would only serve to cheapen Field's considerable prestige. Yet he knew that after every season, unsold premium merchandise sat in storerooms due to overpurchasing or lackluster demand. Markdowns and sales helped to rid them of the slow-moving stock, but displaying discounted items alongside fresh, exciting inventory seemed tacky. Suddenly Harry thought of a strategy for solving both problems. What if they created a "store within a store" that sold bargain goods?

For many years, Field had placed marked-down items in a small area of the store's basement, but the idea had never been promoted. In fact, the "special sales" area was almost a secret. Harry wanted to turn the whole floor into a permanent "bargain basement" that offered the same high-quality goods as upstairs but at a greatly reduced price. Field was a bit dubious, but Selfridge's reasoning made sense to him. It would help them clear out useless inventory, and those people who shopped it might aspire to buy from the regular departments when they could so afford. Some of the old-time employees were scandalized at the proposition. They decried it as cheap and tacky and pandering to the wrong class of customer. One commented that a wealthy woman "didn't want to shop at the elbow of a scrubwoman." Harry insisted that they would maintain the same level of quality and service as throughout the rest of the store, and the word "cheap" would never appear in print. Terms such as "less expensive" and "bargain-priced" would be used instead.

The Marshall Field's bargain basement, later named the "Budget Floor," opened in 1885 and immediately created retail mayhem. Thousands of determined shoppers descended on the department in the first week, snapping up bargains in lace, linens, silks, ribbons and shawls. The wealthy women apparently weren't too put off by the scheme, as many of them joined in the bedlam to snatch up a good bargain. It was such a huge success that it became a permanent department, one that was eventually copied by

Under Selfridge's reign, Field's lowered counter heights and placed merchandise where customers could see and touch the product.

competitors. Selfridge was on a roll, and he knew it. He asked Field for an increase in advertising money, and it was granted. In one year, the store's newspaper space increased by fivefold—going from an expenditure of $5,000 one year to $25,000 the next. Harry wrote much of the copy himself, moving away from Fleming's restrained and dignified advertisements to showy and exuberant layouts that featured pictures of merchandise and bold proclamations about quality and service. He also liked to add inspirational or personal treatises at the top of the ad, in an apparent precursor to his later "Callisthenes" essays. His critics referred to these digressions as "H.G.'s Declaration of Independence," although they did draw the public's interest. But however flamboyant his words, he always insisted on complete accuracy and honesty. Harry was so committed to the premise that he offered a finder's fee of $1 to any sharp-eyed employee who discovered an error or misstatement in any advertisement of the store. He was keenly aware of the power of words and knew how to use them to manipulate customers. Perhaps the best example of this was another of his enduring ideas, the countdown to

Selfridge developed the idea of a Christmas countdown to create a sense of urgency and encourage customers to spend.

Christmas. As the holidays approached, he placed signs throughout the store that urgently proclaimed, "Only __ more shopping days until Christmas!" The subtle pressure induced through this method created a measurable increase in sales, and it has since been copied worldwide.

Although Selfridge definitely had his enemies and detractors, he engendered a strong loyalty from his employees, much as Field had before him. He never publicly criticized an employee; all disciplinary actions were handled discreetly. It is said that if he spotted a dusty counter or display during his daily walks through the store, he would quietly use his fingertip to inscribe his initials "HGS" in the grime, thus leaving the offending employee a silent but pointed reminder of the neglected housekeeping duties. And like Field, he always made time to listen to employees and customers who sought his attention. He once had a conversation with a bright young man named Homer Buckley who worked in the store's shipping department, a crowded and airless place that was derisively labeled the "stink hole." Homer was an observant type, and he mentioned to Selfridge that sometimes frequent customers, whose names he was accustomed to seeing on packing labels, would disappear and no longer place orders. He had pointed this out to his supervisors, but his concerns were shrugged off. Harry was greatly intrigued and asked Buckley to develop a list of such names and write each one a letter under Selfridge's signature inquiring about the loss of patronage. Through this effort, Selfridge was able to communicate with some of the former customers and regain their trust by making amends for the perceived lapse that had driven them away. He immediately moved Buckley out of shipping and created a permanent position for him in post-sale customer satisfaction. Later, Buckley summed up his feelings about his new boss: "He'd inspire you; make you feel you knew how to do things; and he'd do it by talking it out with you, treating you with respect…never talk down to you…I never met a man capable of putting such inspiration into his employees."

In 1889, confident of his successes and perhaps a little arrogant, Selfridge marched into Field's office and requested a partnership interest. Field was stunned at the young man's audacity. Field offered partnerships when he felt they were earned, and although Harry had certainly proven his worth, it was infuriating that he would have the gall to demand the honor before it was offered. Besides, Field knew that Selfridge didn't have the necessary capital to buy a stake. Nevertheless, he had earned a lot of money for the firm and did deserve a share of the profits. "You'll get your partnership, Mr. Selfridge!" rumbled Field. And so, in 1890, Selfridge was awarded a $2/85^{th}$ share, with Field loaning him the $200,000 in required capital. Now Harry was a very rich man, able to mingle easily with the socialites and tycoons in Chicago's upper echelon. He relished the role, spending lavishly on rare books, fine art and furniture. He was a frequent theatergoer, and the newspaper social columns often mentioned his presence—always with his mother at his side—at various opening-night performances. But there was now another woman in his life besides Lois.

Rosalie "Rose" Amelia Buckingham was a very wealthy young woman, the third daughter of Benjamin Hale Buckingham and Martha Euretta Potwin. Rose's grandfather Alvah Buckingham had been a highly successful banker and developer in partnership with his brother-in-law, Solomon Sturges. The firm, Sturges, Buckingham and Company, built the Fulton Elevator at Wolf Point, which was the first grain elevator in the city of Chicago. It warehoused all the grain brought in by Illinois Central Railway until it burned to the ground in 1873. It was rebuilt that same year, and the St. Paul Elevator was added next to it 1879, raising the capacity to 2.9 million bushels and making the company the city's

Rose Buckingham Selfridge with her children, Gordon Jr., Beatrice, Violette and Rosalie.

leading grain warehousing firm. His son, Benjamin, had spent many years as a produce commissioner in New York and Ohio—another family venture—before moving to Chicago to assist in his father's holdings. It was here that Rose was born in 1860. Unfortunately, Benjamin died when Rose was only four years old, but he left behind a substantial inheritance for his wife and children. By her late twenties, Rose had traveled around the world before returning home to establish herself as a successful real estate developer. She had purchased land in Chicago's Hyde Park neighborhood, where she envisioned an upscale artist's community. She commissioned architect Solon Spencer Beman, who had recently completed George Pullman's model housing community, and together they designed and built a beautifully landscaped community of forty-two elegant villas and cottages. Called Rosalie Villas, the homes looked out over the lagoon and prairies, not far from the shores of Lake Michigan. Originally designed as summer residences for the wealthy and artistically inclined, the community included parks, a public hall, the Rosalie Inn and a café called Café Red Roses.

Rose's late father had been a friend of Marshall Field's, and she and Selfridge soon found themselves moving in the same social circles. Harry had never before paid much attention to women, but now he found himself captivated by the attractive and intelligent young woman. She and Harry had a lot in common, apparently including their shared sensitivity about age. In an era when most women were married and with children in their late teens, Rose must have felt that she was approaching spinsterhood as she neared her thirtieth birthday. Like her husband-to-be, she was known to shave years off her age in various documents. But when they married in November 1890, she was thirty and Selfridge was thirty-four. And happily, in what likely could have been a deal-breaker for Harry, Lois heartily approved of her future daughter-in-law.

The wedding was a lavish affair, staged with the hyperbole and pageantry that typified Harry. It was held in the massive Central Music Hall at State and Randolph, just down the street from Field's. More than one thousand of the couple's nearest and dearest friends attended the nondenominational ceremony. In a nod to his bride's ancestry, Selfridge hired a team of designers to create a rendering of the magnificent Ely Cathedral in Cambridgeshire, England, along the main aisle and ceiling of the hall. Thousands of white roses blanketed the stage and filled the air with their delicate perfume, while lilies, chrysanthemums and greenery climbed the pillars. Not content with a simple organist, Harry hired an entire orchestra of harps, organs and strings and a choir of fifty, arranged and directed by Dr. Florenz Ziegfeld, director of the Chicago Musical College. The groom gifted his bride with a stunning and showy blue diamond necklace. Although many in attendance criticized the affair as garish and theatrical, it was pure Selfridge. In another predictable turn of events, Lois—who was now referred to as "Madame Selfridge" since the title of "Mrs." had passed on to Rose—accompanied the happy couple on their honeymoon to Newport Beach, Rhode Island.

Upon their return, Harry and Rose lived for a while with Rose's sister Anna and her husband, Frank Chandler, in their grand home on Rush Street. Eventually, the couple found an elegant mansion on nearby Lake Shore Drive that suited them properly. Lois moved in as well and would live with them for the rest of her life. Soon "Madame" would become a grandmother. Tragically, the couple's first child, a boy named Chandler (who was named in honor of his aunt and uncle), died soon after his birth in 1891. Four more children followed: Rosalie in 1893, Violette in 1897, Gordon in 1900 and Beatrice in 1901.

Rose embraced her role as a wife and mother and turned her attention away from business and real estate to concentrate on hobbies and entertaining. She and Harry had received forty-eight acres of beautiful timbered lakefront property in Lake Geneva, Wisconsin, from Anna and Frank, and it was here that they later built a magnificent mock Tudor-style manor, complete with large greenhouses and extensive rose gardens. It was christened Harrose Hall, in a name derived by combining Harry and Rose. Both were avid horticulturists; Harry cultivated roses and developed a white variety that he named after his mother. Rose was an experienced orchid grower and was rumored to have more than two thousand varieties in her greenhouse. Rose, Lois and the children spent most of their summers on the lake, joined by Harry on the weekends. There was always plenty of family about; Anna and Frank owned a large adjoining estate known as Ceylon Court. Rather than build an ordinary mansion, the Chandlers had purchased an elaborate structure built by the government of Ceylon for the 1893 World's Columbian Exposition and had it disassembled and rebuilt on the shores of their Lake Geneva property. The families greatly enjoyed their time together and entertained lavishly.

Back in the city, Mile-a-Minute Harry was hard at work at Field's looking for the next opportunity to create a sensation. He had been in his glory when Chicago had hosted the 1893 Exposition, which drew participation from forty-six countries. The six-hundred-acre fair brought approximately 27 million people to the city during its six-month run, and Selfridge did his level best to entice each and every one of them into the State Street store. Field's had expanded rapidly in advance of the Exposition, with a new Daniel Burnham–designed nine-story annex to the east of the main store that added 100,000 square feet of retail space. Selfridge worked closely with Burnham—whom he came to call "Uncle Dan"—to fit out the interior of the store, including specialized lighting and other design features. The annex boasted thirteen ultramodern high-pressure hydraulic elevators, new-fangled revolving doors and plenty of lavish appointments, and Field's buyers were ordered to scour the far corners of the globe for the finest merchandise to fill the new space. Selfridge touted the store in a massive advertising campaign as an exhibition unto itself, and visitors poured through to see the wonders of technology and commerce. Irish linen, oriental silks, Persian rugs and Bohemian glass shared space with the newest and most advanced household products made in the United States. Sales at the store skyrocketed, and Field rewarded Selfridge with an even larger share of the profits.

The display department at Marshall Field's created exciting and attractive window displays that encouraged customers to stop and view the latest merchandise.

However, Harry wasn't completely appeased. His salary of $20,000 per year equaled more than $522,000 in today's dollars, and that didn't include his generous partnership profits or other bonuses. But he still wasn't earning quite as much as his old boss, John Shedd. And although Selfridge considered the man a close friend, he had always felt jealous of Shedd. As Marshall Field aged, it was becoming quite clear to Selfridge that Shedd was Field's heir apparent and was being groomed to take over the business when Field retired. Harry wanted more—he wanted to be a senior partner and have the bronze plaques on the building read "Field, Selfridge and Company." It wasn't going to happen. Although he had the greatest respect for Selfridge's talents, Field did not believe that Harry had the business acumen to run the entire operation. Shedd did. Field once called him "the greatest merchant in the United States," and there was no question that Shedd could step into Field's shoes with little disruption in the company. After twenty-five years, Harry knew that it was time to move on.

THE COMPETITOR DOWN
THE STREET

There are six useful things for notable success in business—judgment, energy, ambition, imagination, determination and nerve. But the greatest of these is judgment.
—Harry Gordon Selfridge

Selfridge was now in his late forties and had long surpassed even the most fanciful "supposings" that he and Madame had shared so many decades ago. He was a multimillionaire, had married into an esteemed high society family and was a driving force behind one of the most respected retail emporiums in the world. He owned two mansions—one overlooking Lake Michigan on Chicago's tony Lake Shore Drive and another massive country estate on the shores of Lake Geneva. He had four beautiful children and an adoring wife. And yet it still wasn't enough. Harry had power, but he sought recognition. Money alone could not fill that empty nagging space in the heart of a once-poor lad who had swept floors and delivered newspapers to help put food on the family table. At Marshall Field & Company, he was a giant in the land of giants. No matter what he achieved, he would always share the spotlight with the likes of John Shedd and Field himself.

As Selfridge struggled with his discontent, another merchant down the street was also ready to make a change. David Mayer, of the Schlesinger and Mayer Department Store, was exhausted and at his wits' end. His partner had retired, a massive rebuilding project had drained his capital and he wanted nothing more than to relieve himself of the stress. It was time to seek a buyer for the business.

Horse-drawn wagons and cable cars dodge pedestrians in front of Marshall Field & Company's State Street store.

David had been born in Germany, but his family immigrated to America in early 1852 when David was just an infant. The Mayers were a hardworking middle-class family, and as a child, David attended public school in Chicago. By his early teens, he had quit school in favor of work. What he lacked in formal education, however, he more than made up for with a strong work ethic, a sharp intelligence and the ability to inspire trust and loyalty. While working at a small dry goods store, David befriended another young German, Leopold Schlesinger, and the two excitedly discussed the idea of going into business together.

Leopold had been born in Brotchizen, Germany, in 1842. His family was wealthy, and young Leopold enjoyed the luxury of an extensive education. After he completed his university studies, he traveled to Chicago in 1862 to seek work. His first job was as an office clerk for a small dry goods wholesaler, where he worked hard to learn the trade. Each week, he carefully set aside some of his salary in the hope that he could someday open his own business. When he and David met, he knew that it was time. The two men pooled their resources and in February 1872 opened a small dry goods shop at the corner of Madison and Des Plaines Streets on the west side, in what was once the St. Denis Hotel. At the time, Madison Street was the major east–west route for the horse-car lines, and some thought that it would become the new commercial area since State Street had been largely destroyed in the Great Fire the year before. Business was good for the young men, and they soon opened a second branch farther west on Madison at Peoria Street. The business of Schlesinger and Mayer was positioned to appeal to the middle-class trade—not quite as upscale as what was offered by Field and Leiter but well above the common goods offered by low-priced merchants of the day such as the Fair Store or the Beehive.

The men's partnership was successful and pleasant. They shared many interests, including memberships in the exclusive, private Union League Club and the Standard Club of Chicago. Both organizations were founded in the mid- to late 1800s to promote civic, social and philanthropic interests, and they each contributed greatly to Chicago's cultural and community development. Both Schlesinger and Mayer were active members and gave generously of their resources. In fact, Mayer later attributed their business success to a policy of honest dealings and civic responsibility. But despite the early profitability of their west-side stores, it was becoming apparent that State Street was slowly regaining its prominence as the city's street of merchants. Field's and Carson's had returned, and other merchants were gradually filling in along the rebuilt street. If Schlesinger and Mayer wanted to remain competitive, they would need to find a suitable location near their peers.

In April 1881, the men signed a lease for a portion of the ground-floor space of the Bowen Building on the southeast corner of State and Madison. It was an ideal spot: the commanding and beautiful Parisian-styled façade of the building boldly dominated the intersection and created an image of a fashionable cosmopolitan emporium. This new positioning allowed them to attract a portion of the well-to-do carriage trade from Marshall Field & Company—newly renamed after Levi Leiter's retirement—and yet their merchandise selection and average price points weren't too far out of reach for some of the more bargain-minded shoppers who typically patronized the Fair Store. In fact, the Bowen Building's site was almost equidistant from Field's to the north and the Fair to the south.

Another advantage to the new location was that it sat squarely at the crossroads of the fancy new cable car system that was slowly replacing the old horse-drawn cars. Operated by the Chicago City Railway, the line opened on January 28, 1882, and was just the second cable car line in the country after the famed San Francisco system. Although some cynics doubted that the technology would work in Chicago's frigid climate, it turned out to be surprisingly reliable. It employed a continuously moving loop of heavy cable than ran just below street grade and traced a path from State and Madison east to Wabash Avenue, north to Lake Street, west back to State and south to Thirty-ninth Street. The route was also shared with the Wabash/Cottage Grove line, which continued south and east to Fifty-fifth Street. Later, the service was expanded to many other parts of the city, but it's likely that this original rectangular course of cable spawned Chicago's long-standing nickname for its downtown business district: the Loop.

The new cable cars were a merchant's dream, at least for those whose businesses stood along the route. No matter what the weather, they delivered a steady stream of shoppers right to the doors of Carson's, Field's and Schlesinger and Mayer. All of the businesses profited, but the Schlesinger and Mayer store enjoyed the most prominent location at the junction of the system. This distinction, however, didn't come without a price. In fact, their corner was considered some of the most costly real estate in all of Chicago, with a price of $3,000 per frontage foot by 1890. To remain profitable, they needed to continue expanding in order to generate sufficient revenue to keep pace with the escalating real estate prices. It was no surprise, then, that they quickly stretched beyond their original floor plan. At first, they expanded upward by leasing floors from their upstairs neighbor, wholesaler Clement, Moore and Company. Soon they occupied the entire building and began to acquire additional storefronts adjacent to the Bowen Building to the south on State. As the store grew, the partners commenced a series of remodeling projects in an attempt to give the new additions a unified appearance. By 1890, they had expanded farther down State, and they knew it was time to move beyond their patchwork approach. This time, they would spare no expense and performed a dramatic renovation. Of course, they would hire the best to achieve that goal: none other than the architectural firm of Dankmar Adler and Louis Sullivan.

Adler and Sullivan designed more than 250 buildings during their fifteen-year partnership, employing a style that was both distinctly American and highly functional. In fact, Sullivan's personal mantra was "Form ever follows function," and that philosophy was perhaps best expressed in Chicago's Auditorium Building, the crowning jewel of their long collaboration. The multipurpose building—which still stands today at the corner of Michigan Avenue and Congress Parkway—was completed in 1889 and houses a world-

Construction of the graceful Louis Sullivan–designed store of Schlesinger and Mayer. Selfridge would later buy—and then sell—the business over a span of about three months after leaving Marshall Field's.

class theater with seating for 4,200, perfect acoustics and breathtaking design. An 1890 addition added a 400-room hotel (which now houses Roosevelt University) and 136 office suites. The partners' talents meshed perfectly. Adler was a gifted engineer as well as architect, and he was responsible for the theater's acoustics; its innovative raft foundation, which allowed the massive structure to be built on soft clay; and the auditorium's central air-conditioning system, which made it one of the first public buildings in the country to enjoy such a novelty. Sullivan, on the other hand, was the firm's visual master. An artiste in both talent and disposition, he was an avid student of the writings of Walt Whitman and Henry David Thoreau. He incorporated themes of nature into the ornamentation of many of his buildings, such as intricate scrollwork of vines, leaves and other organic elements that he used to draw the eye upward and enhance the perception of a building's height.

Although the architects created magic in their tall buildings, their personal lives were quite another matter. Adler was short, portly and genial, well-liked and respected by both his clients and the many draftsmen under his employ. Frank Lloyd Wright, a young apprentice of the firm who would later go on to achieve his own considerable fame, described him as a kind and fatherly man who took great interest in his associates' work. He was known to roll up his rumpled shirt sleeves and perch on the edge of a drafting stool, offering advice and encouragement. Adler and his wife had three children (two sons and a daughter) he apparently doted on, as well as a wide circle of friends. By contrast, Sullivan was tall, thin and insular—some would say arrogant—and had little use for his underlings. Although he considered Wright a friend and would sometimes engage him in long philosophical conversations in the quiet at the end of a busy day, Wright recalled that the other draftsmen "might as well have been office furniture" in Sullivan's eyes. Although Sullivan did wed a young woman named Mary Hattabaugh, the couple separated after some years. He had no children and, it seems, few close friends. By most accounts, Sullivan sought solace in the bottle, struggling with a lifelong addiction to alcohol. Many clients found him difficult and temperamental. David Mayer, however, had a great respect for the brooding architect's talent and knew that he and Adler would be the perfect team to renovate Schlesinger and Mayer's beautiful but cramped store at State and Madison.

Adler and Sullivan faced the challenge of increasing the square footage without losing the structure's imposing and distinctive façade. They sacrificed the building's original ornamental corner dome and mansard roof to add two additional stories and topped the now-flat roof with an ornate cornice of cast iron. The dramatically embellished ironwork was painted a brilliant white, and the architects carried the design through the new storefront acquisitions on State, effectively creating the appearance of one large, sleek building. The beautiful curved front of the Bowen Building remained, commanding attention from any passersby and drawing attention to the large display windows that flanked the intersection.

As 1893 approached, though, the nation once again slipped into a deep financial crisis. It began, in part, due to a sudden halt in investments by a large Argentinean bank, which caused a run on gold in the U.S. Treasury. The waves of panic spread throughout parts of Europe, and some foreign investors began to rapidly sell off American stocks. Eventually, nearly six hundred banks across the country failed, several railroads shut down and about fifteen thousand businesses shuttered their doors. Unemployment was rampant; one oft-quoted source estimated that, on average, eighteen out of every one hundred were out of work by 1894, but many areas were hit much harder. New York was said to reach a peak of 35 percent unemployment that year, and in parts of Michigan—including Selfridge's hometown of Jackson—a heartbreaking 43 percent of the population was hungry and jobless. Chicago, in large part because of the World's Columbian Exposition, was spared the worst of it, but the city was not unaffected.

Schlesinger and Mayer enjoyed a steady, if somewhat reduced, stream of business. Their architects, however, were not so lucky. The poor economy led to fewer commissions, and although Adler borrowed money to keep the firm afloat for a while, Adler and Sullivan dissolved their partnership in 1895. Adler briefly accepted a position with the Crane Elevator Company but soon realized his heart was in architecture, and he eventually opened a new practice with his sons. Sullivan struggled to build a solo practice but had some difficulty attracting clients. Frank Lloyd Wright—who had himself been fired by Sullivan in 1893 following an acrimonious dispute over Wright's moonlighting as a residential architect—observed that the client base of Adler and Sullivan had been overwhelmingly loyal to Adler. Only a handful remained with Sullivan after the split, but David Mayer was one of them.

Despite the rocky economy, Schlesinger and Mayer continued to grow their business. In 1896, they purchased a four-story stone-fronted building on Wabash Avenue that backed up against their State Street holdings. The partners knew that the Union Elevated Railroad would soon open an elevated commuter railroad along the avenue, and competitors Marshall Field and Mandel Brothers had already begun to expand eastward to Wabash in response to the limited and expensive footage along State. Mayer retained Sullivan to redesign the building and create an elegant east entrance for the expected throngs of commuters that would transit through the Wabash and Madison station each day.

In the initial stage of the project, Sullivan opened up the façade on the building's first two floors, creating massive plate glass display windows framed by intricate iron scrollwork. The next phase included plans to add six more stories to the original structure, thus creating a commanding ten-story edifice, but for some reason this was never carried out. Instead, Sullivan designed and built a stunning pedestrian bridge that spanned the street from the elevated station to the second-floor entrance of the new Wabash addition. The ornamented steel-girded passage was enclosed with floor-to-ceiling plate glass, which protected shoppers from inclement weather yet allowed them a bird's-eye view of the street below. The roof was a continuous skylight, and electric lights throughout the passageway cast a warm glow that drew shoppers into the welcoming doors of the store. From street level, its appearance belied its strength; it looked to be an elegant corridor of glass suspended by a delicate lacework of ornamental iron. Not surprisingly, it was soon dubbed the "crystal bridge."

In many ways, the merchants of that era defined themselves—and created an aura of success and desirability—through their architecture. The competition to remain fresh and relevant in the public's eye resulted in an almost-constant reinvention of each merchant's physical location. As soon as one store remodeled or added additional sales space, it created a ripple effect down the length of State Street. Thus, when Mandel Brothers began an extensive renovation directly across the street from Schlesinger and Mayer, the partners knew that they had to rethink their plans in order to compete. Perhaps it was time to begin anew. So, in 1898, Schlesinger met with their landlord, Levi Leiter, to discuss the possibility of a brand-new building.

When Leiter had retired from his partnership with Marshall Field in 1881, he had turned his attention to real estate and soon acquired a portfolio of desirable properties, including the site at Madison and State. Typically, merchants leased the land and buildings that contained their stores, but the expense of any new construction fell to the lessee. Having a tenant that was willing to shoulder the cost for a new and improved structure was obviously attractive to Leiter. He agreed to an extended lease and gave Schlesinger and Mayer permission to construct a new building, with a few caveats. The facility had to be at least eight stories tall, completely fireproof and of steel and iron construction. Leiter also reserved the right to approve the final plans. Sullivan was once again offered the commission, and he immediately headed for the drafting table.

The initial proposal was for a twelve-story steel-framed structure to be finished with a façade of marble and bronze. It was an ambitious project with an estimated cost of $1 million, leaving some critics skeptical about whether it would truly come to fruition. Sullivan would also be briefly reunited with his old partner, Adler, who accepted the position of mechanical engineer to design the building's power plant. But before the construction even began, Levi Leiter found himself in desperate need of some quick cash. His son, Joseph, had tried to corner the world wheat market and was for a short time the largest individual holder of wheat in the history of the grain trade. Unfortunately, when Joseph refused to sell some of the desperately needed grain to meatpacker Philip Armour, Armour was incensed. He immediately sent a flotilla of ice-breaking tugs through the frozen lake and north to Duluth and hauled back enough wheat to cover his own needs plus enough extra to flood the market. Joseph's investment crashed, and he found himself $20 million in debt. Leiter had to liquidate most of his assets, including the State and Madison parcel, to help his only son recover from the crushing debt. He sold that property to his old partner, Marshall Field, whose own fabulously successful store sat just one block to the north. Field, however, held a longstanding belief that competition was healthy and necessary, and to Schlesinger and Mayer's great relief, he quickly agreed to allow the project to proceed.

In 1899, work began on a section of Madison Street. The original plans had been revised several times to conform to the city's height restrictions and other building constraints, and the design now called for a nine-story edifice. The construction was scheduled in stages so that the store could continue to operate and generate much-needed revenue, and by early December 1899, the Madison Street section opened its doors to hordes of Christmas shoppers eager for a look at the luxurious and modern facility. The development had been costly, though, and the partners needed some time to recoup before they could begin the next phase.

The project languished until 1902, when Henry Siegel of Siegel, Cooper and Company offered to buy into the partnership. By this time, Schlesinger was worn out from the many years of hard work and decided to retire. He sold his half of the partnership to Siegel, who came aboard as vice-president and chief investor. David Mayer assumed the role of president, and all parties agreed to retain the firm's well-established name of Schlesinger and Mayer. But now, with Siegel's infusion of capital, the planned rebuilding could proceed. By this time, the city council had relaxed height restrictions, and the new partners proceeded with Sullivan's original twelve-story plan for the State Street side. In order to disrupt trade as little as possible, the construction firm of George Fuller and Company devised a method of

Selfridge sold his Chicago business to Carson, Pirie, Scott and Company and shortly thereafter moved to England.

shoring up the original Bowen Building and sinking a new foundation beneath it while business in the store continued as usual. Only after the foundation was complete and the Christmas shopping season was behind them, in January 1903, did they begin demolition of the old building.

The finished structure, which was completed in the fall of 1903, featured a rounded entrance with arched doorways embellished with elaborate iron scrollwork that continued across the first two floors. Glossy ivory-enameled ornamental terra cotta climbed the exterior walls and flanked the wide windows that let sunlight stream far into the interior. The beautiful edifice was reminiscent of an exclusive Parisian department store, Magasins du Printemps, and it brought an air of elegance to the corner that was unlike any of its peers along State Street. Unfortunately, it also came at an astronomical price; the price of construction alone had exceeded $1.6 million due to serious cost overruns, and more interior work was required. The inevitable temporary decrease in sales due to construction had seriously hurt the firm, and Mayer was struggling with a heavy debt load. He had first approached his new partner, Henry Siegel, for additional funding in early 1903 while the work was still in progress, but Siegel was reluctant to invest any more.

Mayer also tried to strike an agreement with Otto Young, who owned the land parcels south of the new store. Mayer envisioned a huge building complex that filled the entire block, but after much negotiation, the deal fell apart. Some say it was because Young would not agree to use Sullivan as an architect, and Mayer refused to be disloyal to Sullivan by turning the work over to Daniel Burnham, Young's preferred architect. In any case, the relationship between the two men turned quite acrimonious, and any future chances for expansion seemed unlikely. Mayer was dead tired of the struggle and perhaps more than a little overwhelmed. He had to find a better solution.

While all this drama was unfolding down the street, Carson, Pirie and Scott was facing its own problems. Although business was quite good, the company had been informed that its soon-to-expire lease for its retail store in the Reliance Building at Washington and State would not be renewed, since the building would be sold to the Hillman's grocery company. Losing a presence on State Street was not an option; the partners knew that they needed to find a new location quickly, but available square footage was scarce, especially for a store of such grand size. David Mayer knew of their predicament and thought that maybe he had the perfect solution. In March 1903, he approached Pirie with a proposal: the two stores could merge at Mayer's beautiful new building, perhaps operating under the name of Carson, Pirie and Mayer. It was a fascinating offer, but quite a drastic step. Carson's board would need some time to consider the options. Mayer, however, was impatient and exhausted. While the Scotsmen were mulling it over, he would continue to cast around for a solution. Little did anyone know that a third player was about to enter the picture and completely change the dynamics.

Of course, that third player was Harry Gordon Selfridge. His timing was perfect; Mayer was more than happy to get out, and he promptly agreed to sell the entire interest in the firm of Schlesinger and Mayer for a reported sum of $5 million. It was early May when Selfridge broke the news to Marshall Field, and perhaps he was hoping for a plea to stay and become a senior partner. If so, he was disappointed. Reportedly, Harry said,

Harry Gordon Selfridge hard at work in his office.

"Mr. Field, I have decided to go into business for myself. I am going to buy Schlesinger and Mayer's interest." After a brief hesitation, Field replied, "Very good, Mr. Selfridge. I hope you are successful." Harry offered to stay until the end of the year, but Field dismissed him abruptly, saying, "No, you can leave tomorrow if it suits you." Some Selfridge biographers have used this exchange to portray Field as a cold and ungrateful old man, but it's more likely that he simply wasn't surprised. Harry had made his displeasure quite clear, and there were few secrets in their social circles. Field might also have felt betrayed. Selfridge had been rewarded handsomely for his talents and had been allowed to proceed with almost any scheme that he fancied. Field had always supported and encouraged him. Of course, Harry must have been hurt that his career of twenty-five years at the store ended so dismissively. It was likely a bittersweet ending for both of them.

In any case, Selfridge quickly traded his partnership interest in Field's for $1.5 million as a down payment on his new store and borrowed the balance from friends and relatives. But no sooner had the ink dried on the contract than Selfridge realized that he was in deeply over his head. He really didn't have sufficient capital to run the business. Almost immediately, he discussed a deal with Otto Young, Mayer's old nemesis, to sell the building and leaseholds to Young and simply lease back the property. The plan would work out well for all involved: Mayer had retired with a sizeable fortune, Young would own most or all of the buildings on the east side of State between Madison and Monroe and Selfridge possessed a beautiful, elegant department store. He immediately installed plaques that read, "H.G. Selfridge and Company" near the entrances and draped banners across the building. As he had done at Field's, he blanketed the town with advertising. On his opening day in June, he climbed to the roof—impeccably dressed in a fancy morning coat and silk hat—and ran up a silken house flag to the accompaniment of a band.

The honeymoon didn't last for long. After just a few months of operating the new store, Selfridge desperately wanted out. He loudly complained that the employees lacked the same work ethic and enthusiasm as those he had employed at Field's, and he quickly found himself overwhelmed and with no one qualified to offer support. "There are a million things to do and nobody to do them!" he grumbled. He also felt "extremely miserable" fighting over customers with his former house. "I feel as if I am competing with my own people," he lamented. So, in desperation, he sheepishly turned to his old rival at Field's, John Shedd, for help and advice.

The next morning, as Shedd pondered the situation, he bumped into John T. Pirie in front of the Field's store. Pirie apologetically admitted that he had been snooping about Field's latest window displays, and with an

Selfridge's store in Chicago lasted only a few months before he sold to Carson, Pirie, Scott and Company.

embarrassed nod, he turned to go. Suddenly Shedd realized that there was a simple solution to everyone's dilemma. He pleaded with Pirie to come up to his office for a discussion. Pirie at first was reluctant, but Shedd soon convinced him that there was an urgent opportunity at hand. It was common knowledge on the street that Carson, Pirie and Scott were seeking new quarters, and with his private awareness of Selfridge's desire to quit the business, he believed he could help broker a deal that would solve both men's problems.

At first, Pirie laughed at the idea. Selfridge had only been in business for a scant few months, and it seemed preposterous that he would already be willing to sell. But Pirie knew that John Shedd was a man of honor and integrity, and it appeared as though he had some insight in the matter. Shedd offered to orchestrate the negotiations, acting strictly as a neutral friend to both parties. Pirie was intrigued and finally agreed to proceed with talks. Shedd picked up the telephone and made arrangements for Selfridge to meet them immediately at the offices of the Illinois Trust Safe Deposit Company. Pirie contacted his son, Samuel Carson Pirie, who was running most of the day-to-day operations of the firm, and asked him to join them.

When the group arrived at the bank a short time later, Shedd quickly secured three conference rooms; he occupied the center room, with Selfridge in the room on the right and the Piries to the left. Within one half hour, the first offer was made: Selfridge would sell the entire business for the $5 million he paid, plus a $250,000 bonus. The Piries countered with an offer of $5 million plus a $150,000 bonus. Shedd dashed from room to room with scraps of paper containing scribbled notes, questions and bids. After a brief flurry of negotiation, they reached a compromise: $5 million plus a $200,000 bonus. Sam C. Pirie accepted by jotting, "Sold, S.C.P." on the latest paper scrap, and Shedd signed with Selfridge's authority, "O.K. Selfridge." When the men gathered to shake hands, Selfridge voiced one concern: although nothing had been signed, he was in the middle of negotiations with Otto Young regarding the sale and leaseback of the property. He feared the possibility that Young might try to enforce their verbal agreement, so he added a caveat to the scrap paper: "O.K. if Young agrees."

The next morning, Otto Young agreed to relinquish any claims, but the Piries weren't having such an easy time of it. The many partners of Carson, Pirie and Scott felt that Sam Pirie had moved too hastily, and they wanted to reopen the negotiations. So once again, all parties trundled back to the same bank offices they had sat in the day before. This time, the room to the left was a bit more crowded. Five partners showed up on behalf of the firm: John T. Pirie, Sam C. Pirie, Robert Scott, George Scott and Andrew MacLeish. The debate was spirited and prolonged. Shedd later observed that "the partners debated the matter with me for two hours…finally it being evident that it was the only opportunity for Carson, Pirie Scott & Company to continue retail business on State Street…[they offered] Mr. Selfridge a bonus of $150,000 which Mr. Selfridge instructed me to accept."

Finally, everyone was happy. Carson, Pirie and Scott had secured a home on State Street in an exquisite building that it would ultimately occupy for more than one hundred years. Shedd was a hero of sorts, garnering profuse thanks from all parties in the transaction. And Mile-a-Minute Harry had walked away from the whirlwind months of legal contracts with a hefty bonus in his pocket. In fact, he was quite proud of himself. For the rest of his life, he boasted that "I am the only man ever to buy a business from five Jews and sell it to seven Scotchmen at a profit."

THE AMERICAN DEPARTMENT
STORE COMES TO LONDON

A store which is used every day should be as fine a thing and in its own way as ennobling a thing as a church or a museum.

—Harry Gordon Selfridge

Harry was bored. In the months since he had walked away from his brief flirtation with department store ownership, he had spent most of his time puttering around his huge estate on Lake Geneva. He spent time with his children, fussed with his roses and attended a few civic meetings here and there in Chicago, but nothing quelled the restlessness he was feeling. Not even his latest expensive amusement, a steam yacht that he could pilot around the lake, held his interest for very long; it soon sat idle at its mooring. He had invested heavily in a gold mine, the Sullivan Creek Mining and Milling Company, but it had turned out to be barren. Perhaps a tour of Europe with his family would fan his imagination.

Before the trip, Selfridge attended a dinner with millionaire Walter H. Cottingham, who had gained substantial wealth as the general manager, and later president, of the Sherwin-Williams Company, a pioneer in the paint industry. Cottingham was in the process of setting up a partnership with the London paint firm of Lewis Berger & Sons, Ltd., and had spent a great deal of time there. Cottingham told Selfridge, "That's the place for you!" Selfridge later recalled, "Cottingham told me that I couldn't miss. They had nothing there to attract shoppers. People only bought when they had to, and then reluctantly." In later years, Harry would claim that he had pestered

Field to open a store in London, but to no avail, and Field's reluctance to expand was a contributing factor to his departure from the firm. There is, however, nothing to support this claim, and none of his contemporaries ever mentioned such a disagreement. Field had opened buying offices across Europe, including his first office in Manchester many years before, and he had strong ties to England. He certainly wasn't averse to foreign locations. In fact, at the time that the Selfridge family arrived in London, Field was already there, marrying Delia Caton, his second wife, at St. Margaret's Church in Westminster.

In any case, Selfridge brooded over Cottingham's words during the voyage to Europe. When Lois noticed his preoccupation, she said, "I suppose you'll open that store in London now." He said later, "It was as if I were speaking to myself, for she was always able to follow my thoughts." Harry replied with a decisive, "Yes!" And although he had seemingly made up his mind, the ghosts of Marshall Field & Company still haunted his thoughts. It has been said that Selfridge approached Field in London in September 1905 with an offer to buy out the business and that Field was considering the proposal. Although it is certainly possible that the men met to discuss business, it is highly unlikely that Field would have entertained any thought to sell. He certainly didn't need the money; his personal fortune exceeded $150 million. In 1905, Field was the largest single taxpayer in the United States. And the store didn't need any direction. Under John Shedd's capable hand, business was thriving. Finally, Selfridge did not have anywhere near enough capital to make such an offer. One theory is that he had the backing of American financier J.P. Morgan, but Morgan was a friend of Field's; if he wanted the store, it's more likely he would have approached Field directly and kept John Shedd at the helm.

But if Selfridge truly believed that there was any chance to purchase his mentor's empire, those hopes were soon dashed. On January 16, 1906, just four short months after his joyful marriage, Field died suddenly during a trip to New York after a brief bout with pneumonia. Chicago grieved, but the wondrous store he had created would live on for another one hundred years and become a defining icon of the city. When it was absorbed by Macy's in 2006, Chicago grieved once more at the loss of its retail identity.

Selfridge had turned fifty years old at the time of Field's death, and he was at a crossroads in his life. He considered returning to Chicago and finding another preoccupation, perhaps in politics. But he saw endless possibilities in London, and he decided to seize them. He once explained to an associate that "the seal of London's approbation is needed for a career

When Selfridge first began to build his store, much of the area he chose was run-down and derelict, filled with stables and factories. Londoners laughed at the crazy American who was opening a grand retail emporium on "the wrong side of Oxford Street."

which would rise above the merely provincial, the local or the national." And there was certainly plenty of opportunity. The European shopkeepers of the era mirrored Chicago's early retail days, before Potter Palmer—and later Marshall Field—turned shopping into a pleasurable activity. Floorwalkers or sales associates would greet customers and immediately steer them to a purchase. Browsing wasn't allowed, or at least not encouraged. Selfridge always liked to tell the story of one of his early visits to a London retailer. Upon entering the establishment, he was straightaway approached by a sophisticated young assistant who inquired in a gentle and refined voice, "What is sir intending to purchase?" Harry replied, "Thank you, but I'm just looking." With a sneer, the clerk quickly dropped his haughty manner and growled, "Then 'op it, mate." It was definitely time for the American department store to come to London.

Selfridge began studying the competition and casting about for a suitable location. He rejected a location on Bond Street because the road was too narrow. He considered a location on the Strand, but the deal fell through. Next he turned his attention to Regent Street, but size restrictions wouldn't allow him to expand. Eventually, a banker friend introduced him to Samuel Waring (later Lord Waring), a wealthy businessman who owned, among other things, a furniture company, a builder's conglomerate and plenty

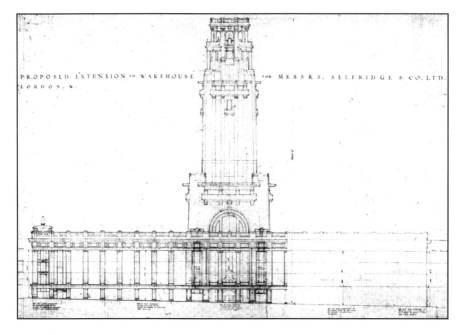

The original plans for Oxford Street called for a massive central tower, but the design was struck down due to London's building height restrictions.

of real estate. Waring held some property on Oxford near Duke Street, which was then a rather derelict part of town that cobbled together small shops, rundown tenements and a gritty pub named the Hope Arms. It was, however, just a short stroll from the Marble Arch and Bond Street stops on the new Central London Railway, London's underground transit system, and not a far distance from the tony mansions of Portman Square. Wealthy women in their fancy carriages often passed by on their trips home from Bond Street. Harry decided it would do quite nicely. His enthusiasm was contagious, and Waring agreed to enter into a partnership. On June 6, 1906, the firm of Selfridge & Waring Ltd. formed with an initial capitalization of £1 million—the equivalent of nearly $135 million in today's U.S. dollar. Selfridge owned 150,006 shares, and Waring held 150,001.

By this time, Harry had already begun to reinvent himself into a proper British gentleman. He was now going by his middle name of Gordon, and he rented a luxurious apartment—complete with a live-in housekeeper and a butler—in Whitehall Court, overlooking beautiful St. James's Park. Abandoning the lighter grays and slightly less formal attire that he wore in Chicago, he now dressed in solemn dark waistcoats and black trousers, always paired with a starched white wing-collared shirt, as well as the obligatory exotic orchid gracing his lapel. His manner was stiff and formal, but he was never quite able to disguise his clipped midwestern American accent. He really wasn't fooling the Londoners, and they watched him with a mixture of disdain and amusement.

In his typical style, Selfridge quickly opened a well-appointed office at 415 Oxford Street across from his chosen building site and commenced with planning. He knew in abstract what the store should look like; in his mind's eye, he envisioned a palace of commerce unlike anything that had ever been built. And when a young American architectural student named Frank Swales appeared at Selfridge's door, Harry's vision came into focus. Swales sketched a concept for an imposing neoclassical building that spanned the entire block, from Duke Street to Orchard Street and from Oxford back to Wigmore Street. It would have a massive central dome as large as St. Paul's Cathedral and would rise six stories above the street. Swales also designed a monogram suitable for such a bastion of capitalism: a stylized British pound sign intertwined with a U.S. dollar sign. Selfridge was ecstatic. He later claimed that he "couldn't bear to be parted" with the drawings, and he carried them everywhere until they were dog-eared and smudged. He sent copies to his old friend "Uncle Dan," the renowned architect Daniel Burnham, who had created the remarkable Marshall Field's annex, and asked him to take on the project.

Burnham had his hands full at the time building John Wanamaker's massive twelve-story emporium in Philadelphia, but he finally acquiesced to Selfridge's pleading. While Burnham set to work to draw up detailed plans from the sketches, Harry began the long process of buying and demolishing properties to clear the site. It certainly wasn't as easy as it had been in Chicago, where most deals could be finalized over a glass of good bourbon and a fine cigar. In London, there were leases and subleases to acquire, wealthy landowners who had to be appeased and handsomely compensated and lots of politics to finesse. Selfridge spent the better part of a year in and out of lawyers' offices and was greatly frustrated in the process. But his worst disappointment was yet to come. While being swept away by his lavish dreams, Harry had never bothered to consult the London Building Act for applicable restrictions. Burnham's elegant plans were summarily rejected by the St. Marylebone Borough Council, in part because the building exceeded height limitations.

Selfridge's partner, Sam Waring, was not amused with Harry's grandiose and reckless approach. After viewing the vetoed plans, he had exclaimed,

The beautiful bronze Art Deco elevators were installed in 1928 and can now be seen at the Museum of London.

"Has the Parthenon pupped?" Burnham, now back to square one after having wasted much precious time, realized that he would need an associate who would be familiar with London's complicated building and safety codes. At Waring's suggestion, he teamed up with R. Frank Atkinson, a young architect who worked in Waring's building company. Together they designed a stately and impressive structure, also in the neoclassical style, fronted by massive columns that hid the modern steel framing. The building stood five stories high with three basement levels and an elegant rooftop terrace. Selfridge insisted that the foundation be strong enough to support additional floors—or perhaps a grand tower—if regulations were ever relaxed. It was built in two phases, with the original section stretching 250 feet along Oxford from Duke Street. It featured nine and a half bays, eleven modern Otis elevators and six elaborate staircases. The second phase, which created an imposing main entrance on Oxford and extended the store all the way to Orchard Street, wasn't begun until 1928.

But shortly after the original excavation commenced in 1907, it was beginning to appear doubtful that the ambitious project would ever materialize. The entire process had been more expensive and complicated than Selfridge had ever imagined, and his vision was proving difficult for the architects to pin down. Burnham's team had already produced approximately twelve thousand blueprints as Selfridge hopscotched from one idea to the next. Waring was running out of patience, and Selfridge was running out of money. To that point, all the capital had been advanced by Harry; their agreement was that Waring would open his checkbook as building progressed. It wasn't progressing very quickly, though. In what was either a desperate attempt to speed up the work or a shameless publicity stunt, Selfridge hired a brass band to play at the construction site on one cold and gloomy November day. He claimed that the music would inspire the workers to pick up their pace, but the neighbors were apparently less than inspired; the police were called on a noise complaint and shut down the act. It also ended the partnership. Waring had seen enough of Harry's shenanigans; he abruptly withdrew from the newly formed company and left Selfridge with what the press would refer to as a "million dollar hole in the ground."

Selfridge put up a brave (some might have said indifferent) front and declared that he would "carry on single-handed," but in truth his back was against the wall. He didn't have the money to proceed, and London's economy was gloomy. Pervasive unemployment and disappointing stock prices had pushed up bank rates and stalled development. He couldn't turn to his friends in America either. An economic crisis there, caused by a failed attempt to corner the market on stocks of United Copper Company, had caused banks to close and stocks on Wall Street to plummet by 50 percent. Without financial backing, he was broke and out of options. To make matters worse, he had recently sold his Chicago mansion to raise capital and moved his wife, mother and children to England and into a splendid

Construction begins on Selfridge's Oxford Street store.

country estate in Kent that he had leased from Waring. It must have been quite a worrisome time for Harry, but he remained upbeat. While his dream languished, he stubbornly continued to plan for his store's eventual opening.

Providence did smile on him, for he was soon introduced to John Musker, a very wealthy gent who had made millions in the tea trade. Musker was also partner in the Home & Colonial grocery stores and was intrigued by Selfridge's concept of an American-styled department store. He agreed to buy the stock shares that had been relinquished by Sam Waring, and he provided a guarantee of £250,000 against Selfridge's debts. Construction on Oxford Street resumed immediately. Harry wanted to open the following March, which meant that nearly 1,500 workers would toil throughout the cold London winter to meet the deadline. It would be the first fully steel-framed commercial building in England. The Chicago School architectural style had popularized the use of steel framing as early as the 1880s, and architect Burnham and his partners, John Root and Charles Atwood, were some of the first to create skyscrapers using this innovative technology. The advantages were obvious; because these buildings were not dependent on heavy brick and stone masonry for support, they could be built taller, and new floors could be added easily. The frame design made it possible to use large plate glass windows, which allowed in plenty of light. In fact, twelve of the store's windows held the largest pieces of plate glass in the world.

And these buildings were much faster to construct and more resistant to fire. Although the London District Surveyors initially displayed skepticism, Selfridge's novel construction impressed the authorities and ultimately led to vast revisions in the 1894 London Building Act.

With construction underway, Harry turned his attention to staffing. He was adamant that it would be a British store with British employees, but he did quietly muster three Americans for his inner circle. C.W. Steines of Chicago joined as merchandise manager, and he and Selfridge immediately headed to Berlin for a week's jaunt to study some of the large shopping emporiums in that city. In spite of his carefully crafted European veneer, however, it seems that Harry intended to stock his store with largely American-made products. Steines quickly headed back to New York, where he purchased a variety of fine leather items, especially large handbags. "There is an increasing call for distinctly American styles, and [we intend] to develop this trade as much as possible," he told the U.S. suppliers in a trade article. William Oppenheimer, an experienced dry goods merchant from New York, was placed in charge of the store's fixtures and layout. Like Selfridge had done at Marshall Field's, Oppenheimer created an inviting layout that displayed goods in the aisles and encouraged browsing. There would be none of the high counters and inaccessible stock that characterized so many other stores.

The last of the American trio was Edward Goldsman, a Chicago visual design artist who had created crowd-stopping windows as the display manager at Marshall Field's. In those years, London merchants simply placed merchandise in their windows, usually shoving the cheapest items to the front in an attempt to entice shoppers. The result was a distracting and unappealing jumble that did little to draw the eyes of passersby. Selfridge's windows would change all that; they would be masterpieces of art and design. L. Frank Baum, Goldsman's mentor, once declared that store windows should "arouse in the observer cupidity and the longing to possess the goods." Harry echoed that sentiment in his own words: "The whole art of merchandising consists of appealing to the imagination. Once the imagination is moved, the hand goes naturally to the pocket." Goldsman sent his assistants out to museums and libraries for ideas and developed carefully themed and orchestrated displays that focused less on specific goods and more on creating an aura of refinement and class that drew shoppers inside to experience the magic. The massive windows, which were lit by electricity at night, created a whole new pastime known as window-shopping.

The remainder of the executive staff was culled from the best and brightest of London's businessmen. There was T.H. Pring, who would serve

Hordes of Christmas shoppers descend on Oxford Street in the 1960s.

as advertising manager; Percy Best, a talented young salesman, who was appointed staff manager; and Arthur Youngman, who was named chief accountant. Frank Chitman, who introduced the first ready-to-wear suits to England, came aboard as manager of men's clothing. Selfridge hired savvy buyers and sent them racing across the continent to procure merchandise and identify new fashion trends in advance of the opening, although some

A wide central aisle and low displays allow shoppers to browse at their leisure.

accused him of terminating the highest-paid of the group once they had filled his store with desirable and uncommon goods. The sales staff, composed heavily of attractive young women, was schooled extensively in the "Selfridge Way," which meant that customers should be treated as guests and must never be hurried or pressured to buy. As he had proven in Chicago, Harry knew that a welcoming environment and helpful, friendly staff would encourage shoppers to linger and thus be more likely to spend. The store would have many of the same amenities as Field's: a library, a writing room, restaurants, a first-aid room and medical bureau, gracious lounges and services of all sorts, including a hairdresser's salon and manicurists. It would even maintain an on-call dentist should a dental emergency ever arise within its hallowed walls. Indeed, a visit to the store could easily provide a day's amusement.

Soon, Selfridge turned his attention to his first love: advertising and promotion. It was a campaign the likes of which London had never seen before. In just the seven days leading up to the grand opening, Harry spent more than £36,000, the equivalent of nearly $5 million in today's U.S. dollars. He attempted to buy the entire front page of the *Times* for his grand-opening announcement, but his request was denied. It hardly mattered; he blanketed the country with expansive and lavish ads, including a full-page announcement drawn by the renowned *Punch* cartoonist Bernard Partridge. He was well aware of the power of the press and courted reporters and editors with lavish gifts and amenities; the store would include a reporters' room furnished with typewriters, telephones, office supplies and a well-stocked bar. Harry once told an associate, "Never quarrel with a newspaper, no matter how right you feel you are. Remember this—a newspaper can always have the last word."

As the store neared completion, tensions rose. Selfridge was adamant that the opening day would be Monday, March 15. Although he now employed a staff of 1,800 and hundreds of contractors, there was still much work to be done. Goldsman had designed a breathtaking window based on the work of French painters Jean-Honoré Fragonard and Jean-Antoine Watteau, only to see his work destroyed when the newly installed sprinkler system malfunctioned. Merchandise displays were set up only to be rearranged countless times in order to achieve just the right effect. The National Telephone Company denied Harry's request to set up an exchange in the store, although it did grant him a rather distinctive number: Gerrard One. It was later memorialized in a British revue act by the rather racy Miss Teddie Gerrard, an Argentinian entertainer, when she sang, "All day long the telephone keeps on ringing hard; are you there, little teddy bear? Naughty, naughty, one Gerrard."

On Sunday, March 14, employees worked throughout the night to prepare for the next day's opening. Just when it had seemed that things were spiraling out of control, Harry called everyone together for a brief meeting. "We are going to open on the day. Don't worry about whether the next fellow will be ready—just make sure that you are!" The question that lurked unspoken in everyone's mind, however, was, "Is London ready?"

THE THEATER OF RETAIL

This is not a shop. It is a community centre.
—Harry Gordon Selfridge

The morning of Monday, March 15, 1909, dawned gray and cold, with the sort of persistent chilly rain that dampened both the body and the spirit. It wasn't enough, however, to dissuade the throngs of shoppers and curious gawkers who gathered impatiently outside the doors of Selfridge's new retail palace. The fine silk drapes that shrouded the massive plate glass windows had been drawn back at early dawn to expose Goldsman's dramatic displays, and the crowd chattered excitedly about what wonders they would see inside. As much for show as for safety, Selfridge had thirty London policemen stationed outside to control the mob.

When the doors opened precisely at 8:30 a.m., the stampede of customers inspired awe and perhaps a little fear in the hearts of the associates who waited pleasantly to serve. More than ninety thousand people passed through the store that day, and upward of 1 million visited in the first week. Unfortunately, the vast majority came to look, not buy. The total proceeds for the first full day of business amounted to a paltry £3,000, barely enough to pay the utility bill. But if Selfridge was worried, he didn't show it. He was thrilled with the crowds and reveling in the spotlight of the momentous occasion. His supreme self-confidence assuaged most of his staff, but not his competitors. Even Frank Woolworth, the American dime store king who was visiting London at the time, said, "Selfridge has spent an enormous amount of money…many Englishmen think he will fail. There seems to be a prejudice against him."

Harry, however, continued to go about his business without a care. He leased the elegantly furnished townhome of the Earl of Yarborough and moved his mother, wife and children to the city from their rented country estate in Kent. The earl's home was filled with exquisite furniture, rare paintings and marble sculptures that lent an air of old money to its inhabitants and played quite nicely into the image that Harry was trying to create. At the store, he decorated his fourth-floor corner office in a manner suitable for British royalty. Overflowing vases of flowers scattered about perfumed the air—Harry did love his flowers—and a single red rose in a crystal vase always sat near his telephone. While still in partnership with Sam Waring, he had commissioned a spectacular custom desk to be built by Waring's furniture company. The massive desk now served as his podium and throne, although due to some lingering bitterness over the partnership's dissolution, Selfridge neglected to pay the invoice for more than three years. On one wall there hung a large portrait of Marshall Field, whom Harry credited as his mentor and often quoted. His staff called him "Mr. Selfridge," or more commonly, "the Chief," and his door was always open to those who desired his attention.

A view down Oxford Street at Selfridge's imposing retail emporium.

Selfridge's offices were always impressive and usually featured vases of fresh flowers.

But a few months after the grand opening, the novelty had worn off and the crowds thinned. A reporter for the *Evening News* wrote that he found some areas of the store "nearly deserted," and *The Draper* cattily referred to the store's initial hubbub as a "nine day's wonder." All the while, Harry continued to plan for expansion. But by summer, even Selfridge had grown uneasy with the meager cash flow. He knew that he had to find a way to get shoppers into his store. First he tried an art exhibit using paintings that had been rejected by the Royal Academy. He postulated that there was hidden genius among these runners-up and invited the public to come and form their own opinion. Traffic picked up slightly. Next, he held huge sales, offering low prices on advertised items. But unlike other merchants of the day, Selfridge's sales were exactly what they claimed to be. It was a common practice to use bait-and-switch tactics back then, and fabulous sale items were always "sold out." In reality, most of the advertised items had never existed at all.

Harry had seen this trick before and had once exposed a competitor in Chicago for the deceit. In that instance, the hapless seller had advertised five hundred pairs of shoes at rock-bottom prices. Selfridge knew that the price was below cost and likely a sham, and so he sent an acquaintance to the store. He later explained what happened: "She was a big, red-headed Irish woman. A six-footer, a real terror. I told her to ask for a pair of shoes at the advertised prices. If they were not forthcoming, she was to kick up a row. Of course…she was told that they were sold out…then she started to shout…the fools began to argue with her. That's just what she wanted. She got behind a counter and defied them to move her. Customers crowded round and listened to her denunciation of the store." Afraid to call the police for fear of the bad publicity, the clerks were powerless. "She kept it up until two in the afternoon, when her voice gave out," chuckled Selfridge.

Although his honest sales were drawing in a bit more business, he needed something more, something spectacular that would have all of London flooding his store. As usual, he found it. On a sunny Sunday morning in July, the Selfridge family had gone motoring and was enjoying a leisurely breakfast at a hotel in Kent when suddenly the place was abuzz with news. A French aviator, Louis Blériot, had made the first powered flight between France and England in a newfangled aeroplane. No one had believed that such a feat was possible, but Bléroit had proven them wrong. Harry later claimed that it seemed to be an omen, and he realized immediately that fate had literally flown an exhibition to him. He ran outside to his driver, leaving his wife and mother behind, and excitedly demanded to be taken to Dover, where the aircraft had ended its voyage in a rather ungainly crash landing. When they reached the field, the aviator was already capitalizing on his achievement: he had erected a makeshift tent over the contraption and was charging admission to the crowd that was quickly gathering. Selfridge rushed over and immediately cut a deal to rent the plane for four days for display in his store. Late that night, a railroad wagon steamed out of Dover with its precious cargo, which was listed on the manifest as "flying machine, damaged."

Upon arrival in London, workmen loaded the plane onto a large horse cart and brought it to the store, where they wrestled it into a hurriedly cleared area of the ground-floor bag and trunk department. Harry had somehow managed to place ads in the next morning's papers, which trumpeted the feat and directed the public to view the "headless bird" now on display at Selfridge's. Some have claimed that there really was no surprise and that Selfridge had actually planned the whole promotion in advance with the aircraft's owners—

MR. PUNCH'S PERSONALITIES.
XXIV.—MR. GORDON SELFRIDGE.

HE sallied from Chicago, Ill.
(Gay go the Gordons to a fight),
Prepared by native "sand" and skill
To put our retail merchants right.

All arts he has, this Mr. SELFRIDGE,
For hustling to the topmost pelf-ridge
(Except the Muse's gifts, and these
Are furnished by "CALLISTHENES.")

A 1926 *Punch* magazine cartoon of Harry Gordon Selfridge. The caption refers to Harry's "Calisthenes" columns that ran in daily newspapers for nearly thirty years.

assuming, of course, that Blériot was successful. That would certainly explain the ease with which everything fell into place, but with Harry, it was always difficult to separate fact from fiction.

In any case, it was precisely the boost that the store needed. By opening time, long lines were already forming around the building. To the delight of the crowds, Blériot himself made an appearance that afternoon, accompanied by his lovely wife. Selfridge needed to hire policemen to guard the exhibit and set up barriers to stop the curious from causing any further damage. Flying machines were such a novelty that most people didn't even understand how they operated; Harry helpfully placed a sign by the front that explained how the "aeroplane flies this way." Over the four days that the plane remained at the store, more than 150,000 people came to gawk, and many did stay to buy. Slowly, Londoners were starting to warm to Selfridge's idea of the department store as entertainment. Harry later bragged that he "made the store the third biggest attraction for sightseers in London," bested only by Buckingham Palace and the Tower of London.

Although sales were steadily improving, the store was far from profitable in its first few years. Selfridge soothed his nervous shareholders by paying dividends out of his own pocket to make up for the shortfall. Using his considerable charm and powers of persuasion, he was eventually able to sell even more shares in the company, and by its third year, the store was well capitalized and out of immediate danger. Selfridge immediately bought sixteen more buildings on the block to begin expansion. He seemed unstoppable, but he was much more than a simple showman; he had an unerring instinct for publicity and was able to turn almost any event to his advantage. When Edward VII died suddenly, the entire store was draped mournfully in black crepe. For the coronation of King George V and Queen Mary, Harry sought advice from the Royal College of Heralds before once again draping the façade, this time in deep crimson with gold fringe. Each section displayed the king's monogram embroidered with gold thread, and other adornments celebrated previous monarchs. But his major coup was much craftier. He solicitously invited young members of the royal family— the children of the Duke of Teck—to view the royal procession from a high balcony at Selfridge's. As the king's coach passed, the king and queen smiled and bowed to the waving children, appearing for all the world to be bestowing their implicit approval on Selfridge's palace.

With growing acceptance and growing sales, Harry became a bit more daring. After a trip to Paris, he moved ladies' cosmetics and fragrances to a featured location at the front entrance, where they have remained ever since.

Women of the era had rarely before used more than a moisturizing ointment and fine face powder that would be sold discreetly in the pharmacist's department. Rouge and bright lipstick were considered appropriate only for stage makeup or women of ill repute. Selfridge's changed all that. "I helped emancipate women. I came along just at the time when they wanted to step out on their own. They came to the store and realized some of the dreams," said Harry. Emboldened by the feminist movement and encouraged by early beauty pioneers such as Helena Rubinstein, the ladies of London began to experiment with cosmetics. Even the most virtuous among them might sneak a little dusting of rouge or a subtle lip stain. Soon eye makeup arrived, and women were darkening their lashes and smudging kohl along their lids. Harry even created some fragrances, including the alluring and extremely popular Lily of the Valley. Women delighted in the new scents and products, and the beauty department was soon one of the busiest in the store. Whatever fashion dictated, it could be found at Selfridge's.

Of course, Harry didn't want his customers to be limited to what they could carry. Like Field had done before him, he set up a delivery fleet that consisted of fifty horse-drawn vans, later replaced by sixty-five Halley petrol vans and eleven electric Edison vans that delivered throughout London three times per day. A lady would make a purchase, and it would be quickly whisked away and delivered to her front door within hours. Not only did the ubiquitous vehicles perform a service to customers, but it would also be impossible to pass a day without seeing one or more of these traveling reminders of the great store. They served as a satisfactory form of advertising. And the delicious anticipation of seeing one pull up to the door kept the excitement flowing. Selfridge was slowly but surely imprinting his name on the minds of British shoppers.

He also brought along other successful ideas from his days at Field's. It wasn't long before a "bargain basement" appeared, and London housewives reacted with just as much enthusiasm as their counterparts across the Atlantic. As in Chicago, his competitors sneered until they saw the undeniable success of the concept. Next, he added a book department. Harry had always loved books and had collected fine volumes for many years. In his typical hyperbolic style, he advertised it as the "biggest bookstore in the world," and it carried everything from current literature to historic texts, including sixty thousand copies of a velveteen-covered *Book of Common Prayer* that quickly sold out. But he wasn't content with simply carrying published works; Selfridge's soon began to publish books under its own imprint: *The Holy Bible*, the *World Atlas*, a complete set of the works of Shakespeare and a dictionary all appeared

Selfridge's claimed one of the largest book departments in the world, filled with everything from the latest novels to fine antique volumes.

and were snapped up immediately by shoppers. A helpful volume entitled *The Good Wife's Cook Book* provided women with tried-and-true recipes that would perhaps appease a hungry and irate husband after the lady of the house had frittered away most of her day shopping.

Another new feature that drew crowds was a pet department. It was operated by Miss Frances Simpson and carried live animals and a grand selection of pet supplies. Selfridge loved Pug dogs, so of course Pug puppies

Shoppers fight for bargains at a huge winter sale at Selfridges London.

were often available, along with aquarium fish, canaries, budgies, colorful parrots and kittens. In one instance, Harry used the pet shop to pull off one of his grand schemes. When the new Japanese ambassador to Britain planned a visit, Selfridge commanded his display staff to create an authentic Japanese water garden running the length of the grand dining hall. After inspecting the breathtaking display, he decreed that it wasn't complete, as there were no fish swimming among the water lilies. The designers were momentarily taken aback—there was no way to find traditional koi on such short notice. Not to let down the Chief, they scrambled to the pet department and grabbed buckets full of fancy goldfish. Harry was briefly mollified, until the fish began floating belly-up at an alarming rate. Apparently, the paint that they had used to create the peaceful blue pond was poisoning the water. In a desperate attempt to save the day, he sent staff members scrambling to the sports department to bring back a dozen bicycle pumps in an attempt to aerate the water and revive the fast-fading creatures. Unfortunately, it didn't work, and they had to quickly dispose of the bodies before the diplomat's arrival. Luckily, the ambassador never took his eyes off the exotic hula dancer who was providing entertainment; the fish weren't missed.

By the time World War I began its deadly siege in Europe, Selfridge had bought out John Musker's shares and was now the sole owner of a massive enterprise that employed 3,500 employees who attended to 160 departments. Roughly 500 of those employees left to fight the war, and many never returned. Women began to take over many of the jobs frequently performed by men; they drove delivery vans and even shoveled coal into the boilers. Harry was determined not to let the dark cloud of war drive down commerce. He boldly declared, "Business as usual!" and began an ambitious campaign of advertising and promotions. The same month that war was officially declared, Selfridge's hosted a Scientific and Electrical Exhibition in the store's Palm Court. Visitors could watch the latest wireless telegraphs transmit and receive messages from Paris. There were demonstrations of X-ray technology and other scientific breakthroughs. One of the most amazing displays was a new invention by Archibald Montgomery Low.

Low, who used the honorific "Dr." even though there was some question of his credentials, was a brilliant engineer who authored forty scientific books and eventually became known as the father of radio guidance systems for his later work on guided rockets and torpedoes. In 1914, his latest project was known as the TeleVista, and the crowds at Selfridge's were astounded. This device allowed handwriting, drawings and some still camera images to be sent over the telephone wires and displayed on a distant screen. He called it "seeing by wireless." But Dr. Low wouldn't be able to further develop this precursor to television, and it would later be improved by a Scottish inventor named John Logie Baird, who named his device the "telewriter." Baird gave his first public demonstration of his telewriter's wireless moving images at Selfridge's in March 1925 in another fantastic exhibition.

In 1914, Low was instead called to war by the Air Ministry, which had requested his skills to design a pilotless plane with an explosive warhead. Although his trials were promising, the war ended before a fully functional model was produced, and the government lost interest in the project. The Germans, however, were more than interested in his ideas and realized how devastating they would be in war. This led to two assassination attempts on Low's life. In the first, an unknown gunman fired shots through his office window, but the bullets missed their target. Later, a visitor with a slight German accent offered him a smoke; Low took the cigarette but didn't light it. A later analysis showed that it was spiked with a lethal dose of strychnine.

It wasn't unusual for Selfridge to bring the latest technology to the public. One promotion during war years featured a futuristic all-electric kitchen equipped with the newest labor-saving appliances. He loved the cutting-edge products and was inevitably the first to feature them. While Harrod's and other prominent British retailers saw sales slip during the war, Selfridge's profits actually increased. Although prices were rising steeply, Harry always kept his prices below the Board of Trade figures. Of course, he never failed to advertise that fact in all of the daily newspapers. He held dozens of special merchandise sales in the store, including a straw hat sale, a fur sale, a soap sale and a special opportunity to purchase Serbian war trophies. Harry also used his wizardry in an act of patriotism: he set up a station in the Palm Court for the sale of war bonds and offered cash prizes for those who purchased them in-store. He raised £3.5 million in the sale of more than 300,000 bonds, at an out-of-pocket expense to himself of £11,364. It was costly, but the publicity and resultant increase in store traffic made it worthwhile. But he was also well aware of the stress and anxiety being faced by his employees during those difficult war years, and he did what he could to maintain morale. He promised to maintain his staff at full wages and to provide returning soldiers with their old jobs. For this, the *Daily Express* cheered, "Bravo Selfridge!" in an editorial.

Volunteers staff tables in Selfridge's during recruitment drives.

But despite his natural optimism, by 1918 Harry was growing deeply concerned about supply shortages and the disruption of trade due to the ongoing conflict. In April, he boarded a transatlantic liner for a trip to America to discuss some of these challenges. Shortly after his arrival, however, he received word that his wife, Rose, was ill and that he should return home immediately. Although a deadly flu pandemic was raging across the world, ultimately killing an estimated 100 million people, news of the outbreak and its severity was greatly suppressed by wartime censors in an effort to maintain morale. This flu was particularly lethal; although most strains of influenza affect a disproportionate number of children, the frail and the elderly, this strain—identified in later years as H1N1—attacked healthy young adults. Rose Selfridge would become one of its victims, succumbing to the virus in May 1918.

Harry was absolutely devastated. In spite of his well-known extramarital dalliances, he truly adored his wife and was inconsolable at her loss. Later that same year, his daughter Rosalie married Serge de Bolotoff, a Russian prince, and Gordon Jr. joined the American forces in London. It was only Harry; his mother, Lois; and the remaining children puttering about the Berkeley Square mansion. It must have been a difficult time for Selfridge, but he immediately turned his attention back to his growing empire. Construction began on the western extension on Oxford Street that would ultimately result in a store frontage of 516 feet, making it the longest commercial building in the world. He also began planning to build a massive castle on land he owned in Hengistbury Head, but uncharacteristically, that project never came to fruition. Harry was nearing seventy years of age, and it seemed that nothing would slow him down. Since he had now built his London store to dramatic proportions, he was eager to expand across England. He began an aggressive buying campaign to acquire smaller competitors. Between 1918 and 1929, Selfridge's & Company purchased sixteen stores, including Bon Marche, Cole Brothers and Blinkhorns. Financier Jimmy White advised Harry to restructure his business, and in 1926, Selfridge's Provincial Stores was formed to incorporate the new locations. Gordon Jr., now back from the war, was named managing director of what was soon the largest retail group in Europe. Now father and son were both multimillionaires, with no limits in sight.

The new acquisitions didn't slow down promotions on Oxford Street. The rooftop terrace featured gardens, cafés, a miniature golf course and a gun club exclusively for women. When the General Strike of 1926 occurred, followed closely by the American stock market crash of 1929, the British

Above: The rooftop gardens on the Oxford Street store at various times held a shooting range, miniature golf, restaurants, elaborate parties and fashion shows.

Right: Gordon Selfridge Jr. in 1926. This same year, he was named managing director of Selfridge's Provincial Stores.

Selfridge in London, 1921. He was sixty-five years old in this photo and already had garnered fame as the "Earl of Oxford Street."

economy tumbled and put 2.5 million people out of work. Harry responded by making a daring move that left his competitors dumbfounded: he slashed prices throughout his store by 10 percent on general merchandise and 5 percent on groceries. The sale, which lasted five months, was backed by a massive ad campaign, and the resultant crush of customers broke all previous sales records. He claimed that his motive was "to try and bring down the general cost of living." In any event, he had finally gained the acceptance he so desperately craved; he was now as much a part of London as Big Ben. It came as no surprise when he was memorialized in a little ditty performed by Gwen Farrar and Norah Blaney in the musical *The Punch Bowl*: "Mr. Asquith now is an Earl, Oxford is his street. But Mr. Selfridge still remains The Earl of Oxford Street."

THE EARL'S DOWNFALL

The best way to handle the fair sex is to let them have their own way.
—Harry Gordon Selfridge

Harry was a man of hard desires; his love of commerce drove him to achieve what most men couldn't even envision, but it was his love of decadent pleasures that ultimately drove him to destruction. He was also a man of contradictions; although he was a prodigy at creating wealth, he seemed to have very little notion of its value. He spent it as rapidly as he earned it, renting luxurious properties instead of building a home and buying all the superficial trappings of affluence without creating any lasting security for himself and his family. "He seems to enjoy the sensation of debt," harrumphed a banker when discussing the perpetually overdrawn status of Selfridge's accounts. In many ways, wealth seemed to be nothing more than an ill-fitting costume for Selfridge. He longed for acceptance and respect but seemed to believe that it could be bought just like the glamorous merchandise with which he filled his stores. And this was perhaps most evident in his legendary affairs.

Harry's name has been linked to a long parade of beautiful and famous women: dancer Isadora Duncan, ballerina Anna Pavlova, author Elinor Glyn and Syrie Wellcome, the wife of pharmaceutical millionaire Henry Wellcome. Although Harry had enjoyed many brief indiscretions during his marriage to Rose, his involvement with Syrie was perhaps the first of his rather public—and costly—entanglements. Henry Wellcome and Harry Selfridge

Selfridge had a lengthy affair with actress Gaby Deslys, even moving his family to the country so that he would be free to squire his mistress about London.

were fellow Masons who traveled in the same social circles, where a flirtation between Selfridge and Syrie quickly escalated into a tempestuous affair. She separated from her husband, and Selfridge set her up in a lovely house in York Terrace West. Their on-and-off relationship was never exclusive, however, and if Rose had any inkling of her husband's philandering, she never let on. Henry Wellcome, who was no doubt embarrassed by his wife's well-publicized romances, eventually sued for divorce when Syrie became pregnant with novelist William Somerset Maugham's child. The two married in 1917 when her divorce was finalized, but Maughan was a bisexual who much preferred men to the company of his new wife. Syrie divorced him after eleven years of a mostly distant marriage and went on to become a famous and well-respected interior designer in her own right.

In 1912, while his affair with Syrie was cooling, Selfridge met Gaby Deslys, a beautiful French singer and actress, and became completely smitten. She was well known for her racy shows and sultry dancing, sometimes scandalizing the audience by stripping to her underwear on stage. Shortly before she met Harry, Deslys had captured the heart of King Manuel II of Portugal, who gifted her with an extravagant pearl necklace worth $70,000 before he was deposed in 1910 and exiled to London. She continued to see the ousted monarch occasionally, but she was quick to realize that the real money lay with Selfridge. As he had done with Sylvie, he leased Gaby a stately house in Kensington Gore and filled it with the finest goods from his store: linens, silver tea sets, fine bone china, leaded crystal and Persian carpets. Each day, a Selfridge's store van would rumble up to the door and deliver a huge basket of flowers, food delicacies and fine wine, although Harry himself was a teetotaler. Selfridge's store became Deslys's personal treasure chest; she waltzed through the aisles, picking up whatever caught her fancy and charging it to "the Chief's" personal account. Harry quickly sent Rose and the children to live in the country at Highcliffe Castle so that he could openly squire Gaby about London. One of his friends observed that "he was a genius from 9am until 5pm but a fool at the weekends."

There is little doubt that his paramours placed enormous demands on both his emotions and his assets. A.H. Williams, a longtime associate of Selfridge's, told the story of a missing dog crisis. One afternoon, when Gaby was breezily plundering the store, she returned to her white Mercedes to find that her pampered little Chihuahua had gone missing. She immediately rushed to Selfridge's office and tearfully begged him to find her pet. "Instantly, the entire Selfridge organization was swung into the chase," recounted Williams. The store's delivery teams were dispatched to scour the neighborhood, and a large reward for the pup's return was posted in all the evening newspaper editions. Harry called the police, repeatedly, for any sightings. The publicity and advertising department jumped into the fray, printing hundreds of "Lost" posters and blanketing the area. Williams remembered Selfridge sitting in his office "like a general commanding an army." "This is a serious business, Williams. The dog must be found!" he thundered. When the wayward canine hadn't turned up by daybreak, Harry doubled the reward and his efforts. "[That morning]…he was again at his desk in the role of generalissimo of Operation Dog," said Williams. Happily, a young servant girl had found the hungry pooch the night before, and thinking it was a stray, she had fed it and brought it in from the cold. When she heard about the massive search, she rushed over to Selfridge's with the dog in her arms, where she was handsomely rewarded. Harry immediately scooped up the animal and raced to the Kensington house and, presumably, to a rare display of Gaby's appreciation.

Harry Gordon Selfridge in his later years, which were marred by an obsession with gambling and gold-digging women.

But it seemed that whatever he gave was never enough. By some estimates—in addition to what she took from his store—he spent tens of thousands of pounds on jewelry and other gifts for her at the Cartier shop in the Rue de la Paix, London's exclusive shopping district. She adored pearls, and in a possible attempt to best the former Portuguese king, Harry bought her a string of rare black pearls as long as her height. Another little offering was a stunning diamond necklace with black and white pearl drops set in platinum. And Gaby loved hats, especially dramatic feathered creations adorned with exotic parrot and flamingo feathers. Sir Cecil Beaton, an English fashion photographer and costume designer, once referred to Deslys with her hats as "a human aviary." So vast was her collection that on an Atlantic crossing, she needed to book an extra cabin just to hold her headgear. And Selfridge never failed to indulge her every whim. Unfortunately, it was at a time when the store was expanding rapidly, and every penny of capital was needed to finance the construction. The board of directors watched apprehensively as Harry spent money as though there was no tomorrow. And it would only get worse.

In 1919, Gaby was diagnosed with a severe throat infection caused by the "Spanish flu" pandemic, the same virus that had killed Rose Selfridge the previous year. She underwent several surgeries—twice without anesthesia—as doctors attempted to cure her, but they were hampered by her insistence that they not scar her neck. Eventually, complications arose, and she died in Paris in 1920. Harry, meanwhile, had been entertaining a series of fresh beauties and spending a lot of time at casinos, often losing quite heavily. Also that same year, he and his mother hosted a massive and elaborate Whitsun fête at Highcliffe Castle that drew 5,000 attendees and cost a veritable fortune. Special trains at Bournemouth and Southampton carried the guests to the countryside, where they enjoyed brass bands, a beauty contest and a jazz dancing competition. And the following year, Violette Selfridge was married to French vicomte Jacques Blaise de Sibour Jr. in a lavish ceremony that was attended by 1,200 guests. Harry's salary of £40,000 per year would hardly have covered these extraordinary expenses; instead, he was drawing more and more money from the store.

Selfridge's daughter Violette, later known as Vicomtesse Violette de Sibour after her marriage to Vicomte Jacques de Sibour, son of a French nobleman.

Selfridge's friends and associates could do nothing to stop his inexorable slide into excess. If there was any stabilizing influence left in his life, it would have been his beloved mother, Lois. Sadly, in February 1924, Madame Selfridge passed away from pneumonia at the age of eighty-nine. Harry quickly descended into a world of self-destructive choices that would define his later years. The previous summer, he had attended a revue at London's infamous Kit Kat Club with his daughter Rosalie. Among the performers was a pair of identical twin sisters from Hungary named Jancsi (Jenny) and Roszica (Rosie) Deutsch. Billed as

Harry Gordon Selfridge with his daughter Violette in New York, 1934.

the "Dolly Sisters," their vaudeville act included mirroring each other's moves in a slow, symmetrical dance routine while dressed in astoundingly extravagant costumes of fur, feathers and glitter. The sisters were beautiful: they possessed a flawless complexion, glossy chestnut hair and almond-shaped eyes that gave them the appearance, according to one stage producer's wife, of "cute little dollies," and the name stuck. Harry was enthralled. He was soon squiring them about town and funding their lavish lifestyle. And lavish it was.

The Dolly twins, Jenny and Rosie, are largely credited with contributing to Selfridge's downfall. He covered their massive gambling debts and showered them with expensive gifts.

The twins had learned at an early age that they could make wealthy men weak with their charms. The Deutsch family had emigrated from Hungary to the United States when the girls were just twelve years old, and by the time they reached their eighteenth birthday, they had performed on Broadway and in the famed *Ziegfeld Follies*. "You can't do much, but you're cute," Florenz Ziegfeld reportedly told them. One of their first conquests in New York was "Diamond" Jim Brady, an American financier and philanthropist who was known for his remarkable appetite for both expensive food and diamonds. Restaurateur George Rector once described Brady as "the best

25 customers I ever had," and it was claimed that he would eat as much as ten people at any meal. He also loved jewels, especially diamonds, and had an extensive collection; this was apparently a lust that he shared with the Dollies. He lavished them with expensive jewelry and introduced them to the world of high-stakes gambling at casinos and racetracks. Although Rosie later claimed that their relationship with Brady was strictly platonic, the lovestruck multimillionaire once presented them with a shiny new Rolls-Royce, wrapped in ribbons and parked behind a theater where the girls were performing. Their penchant for wealthy suitors was so well known that in 1918 they starred in a silly comedic film named *The Million Dollar Dollies*, which was written exclusively for them by director Léonce Perret. Shortly thereafter, they moved on to London, where they performed a sultry Persian dance accompanied by a group of trained dogs. The act's name? "The Dollies and their Collies."

Selfridge, it seemed, lost all control of his urges when he met the twins. His gifts to them were extravagant, even when compared to the largesse with which he'd showered Gaby Deslys. He favored Jenny, but according to most accounts he was intimate with both. The girls shared his love of gambling, and the trio was a common sight at casinos in France. Most of the time, he would perch stiffly on a stool behind them at the baccarat table, indulgently handing over a constant stream of F1,000 notes. Their arrangement was simple: the twins were allowed to keep all their winnings, and Selfridge would cover their losses. They played ruthlessly and recklessly—after all, they had nothing to lose. Once, after a disastrous night in which they tallied heavy losses, Harry sent over a diamond bracelet for Jenny and a pearl one for Rosie, so that his "dear girls" wouldn't be sad. Thelma Furness, the Viscountess Furness, spotted Jenny at a casino in Cannes and exclaimed, "I have never seen so many jewels on any one person in my life. Her bracelets reached almost to her elbows. The necklace she wore must have cost a king's ransom, and the ring on her right hand was the size of an ice cube."

Of course, the sparkling gems weren't just limited to jewelry. In one gauche show of affection, Selfridge chose two identical and exquisite four-carat blue diamonds at Cartier and had them set into the shells of two small tortoises for the girls to keep as pets. And it wasn't just Harry who draped the girls in diamonds. Jenny and Rosie would sometimes hand their jewels over to a friend for safekeeping and then appear at the gaming tables looking distressed and heartbroken. Eventually, some wealthy gent would inquire about their misfortune. The twins would then gaze tearfully into the man's eyes and tell him that they had lost everything—"even my last bracelet!"

The breathtaking *Queen of Time* sculpture, created by artist Gilbert Bayes, was unveiled in 1931 over Selfridge's Oxford Street entrance.

Jenny would sniffle. More often than not, some fancy and expensive trinket would soon come their way.

Selfridge, however, seemed completely oblivious to their manipulative ways. He begged Jenny repeatedly to marry him, but she always managed to keep him at arm's length. He showed his adoration in every possible way; knowing that she loved ice cream, he had a fresh batch flown to her each day from London to Paris by private airplane. He also supplied regular rations of fresh chicken breast for her pampered Pomeranian. By 1927, the sisters' popularity was beginning to fade, and to the surprise of their remaining fans, they announced their retirement from show business. Rosie married Mortimer Davis Jr., heir to a vast tobacco fortune, but the marriage lasted just a few years. In 1931, she finally found her one true love: Irving Netcher, whose family had made their fortune with a Chicago department store named the Boston Store. The couple traveled the world, and Rosie never worked again.

Jenny, however, flitted aimlessly from one idea to the next. She decided to open her own couture house in Paris—financed, of course, by Selfridge. It was a failure, and she became even more depressed and restless. It didn't help that she was separated from her sister for the first significant time in their lives and feeling quite lonely. On a whim, she adopted two five-year-old Hungarian war orphans, Klari and Manzi, and tried to pass them off as twins, claiming that they would be the next-generation Dolly Sisters. The youngsters were often seen in tow behind Jenny and Harry as they visited the casinos. By this time, it was estimated that she had squandered more than £5 million of Selfridge's money; in truth, the amount was likely much greater. His personal finances were in shambles, and he had been neglecting the store that he so loved. At a 1932 meeting of shareholders, it was discovered that profits were down, and the managing director, H. Gordon Selfridge, owed the store approximately £155,000 in monies that he had taken out over the previous year. "I will reduce the matter as soon as possible," he promised, but it was a promise he couldn't keep. In fact, from 1926 to 1935, he spent an estimated £2 million, much of it in an effort to win the affections of Jenny Dolly. According to some accounts, he even offered to pay her millions to marry him. But while Harry struggled with his unrequited love, Jenny continued to see other men.

One of her flings was with a French pilot named Max Constant, who was reputed to have unsavory connections to local gangsters. He was seven years younger than Jenny and quite dashing. One fateful morning in March 1933, the couple was returning to Paris when Constant lost control of the sports car he was driving and crashed into a grove of trees. Jenny was seriously injured; she suffered a skull fracture, a punctured lung and life-threatening internal injuries, and the right side of her face was horribly disfigured. It took dozens of costly operations by plastic surgeons to restore her beauty, and she was forced to auction off most of her beloved jewels. Selfridge paid for what he could, but he was nearly bankrupt himself by that time. And although Jenny fully recovered physically, she never recovered emotionally; she later described herself as "a broken shell." She moved to Chicago to be near Rosie and entered into a brief marriage with a wealthy attorney named Bernard Vinissky, but they quickly separated. She then took her children to California, where she rented a Hollywood apartment and tried to rebuild her life. But in 1941, while her girls played on the beach, Jenny wrapped the

Harry Gordon Selfridge escorts Marcella Rogel, his daughter Violette's friend, from a TWA Sky Chief on a trip to Los Angeles. It was rumored that the two carried on a brief romance.

sash from her dressing gown around her neck and hanged herself from a curtain rod in her living room.

After Jenny left for Chicago, Selfridge, who was now nearing eighty years of age, continued with a string of minor affairs, including a brief dalliance with tennis star Suzanne Lenglen, nearly forty-five years his junior. Later, he was linked to the beautiful actress Marcelle Rogez. Whether these affairs were intimate, or just a lonely old man showering his objects of desire with gifts, is a matter of dispute. In any case, he continued to spend money—both his and the store's—with a vengeance. In May 1935, Harry adorned the store lavishly for the Silver Jubilee of George V and Queen Mary. The theme was "Empire," and Selfridge commissioned an eighty-foot-tall statue of Britannia, flanked by golden lions, to be mounted on the store's roof. The decorations were so over the top, so ostentatious, that one of the store's major shareholders, the Prudential Assurance Company, knew that they had to act quickly to stem the financial bleeding. They quietly installed H. Andrew Holmes, an ex-banker and well-respected financial turnaround wizard, to a position on the board. Even Gordon Jr. welcomed the move. He had been growing increasingly concerned with his father's foolhardy mismanagement of the firm's cash and yet didn't know how to rein him in. But Holmes did.

During Holmes's brief time at Selfridge's, he had seen enough to know that Harry had to go. Each cause for celebration in London resulted in extravagant decorations and opulent parties that drew crowds but did not increase sales. Author Gordon Honeycombe, in describing the massive two-ton rotating globe and towering silver statue of Mercury that adorned the store in celebration of its twenty-seventh birthday, summed it up succinctly: "What had once been grandiose was becoming gross." Harry was also becoming increasingly difficult and autocratic. Holmes noted that "Selfridge wanted to go on being king of his own castle, even though it was beginning to tumble." Harry, however, was undeterred by any concerns expressed by the board of directors. He cheerfully boarded the *Normandie* for a trip to America, with the intention of visiting old friends and—more importantly—raising funds to shore up his desperate financial position. He expected a hero's welcome but was instead greeted with chilly reserve. News of his chronic gambling and fiscal irresponsibility had already reached his former

Opposite, bottom: "Blackout accessories" were sold extensively during the war. Because all city lights were extinguished during nighttime hours to hinder air raids, Londoners dressed themselves—and their pets—in white apparel to make seeing one another in the dark a bit less difficult.

During the war, Selfridge's windows often displayed maps and updates about the progress of Allied efforts. This one, entitled *How Italy Lost Her Empire*, was sponsored by the Ministry of Information.

A Christmas tree purchased by the YMCA through its "Gifts to Home League" is loaded into a van in 1944. It is destined for the family of Trooper Devereux, who is away fighting the war.

acquaintances, and no one was about to loan him a dime. He returned to England empty-handed.

As the Second World War began, the British economy slumped, and sales at Selfridge's were the weakest they had been in many years. Holmes decided that it was time to make his move. Gordon Jr. had disappeared on an extended trip to America after an acrimonious dispute with his father over finances, but Harry seemed completely oblivious to any troubles with the store. He must have been taken by surprise that September morning when the members of the board of directors suddenly assembled in his office.

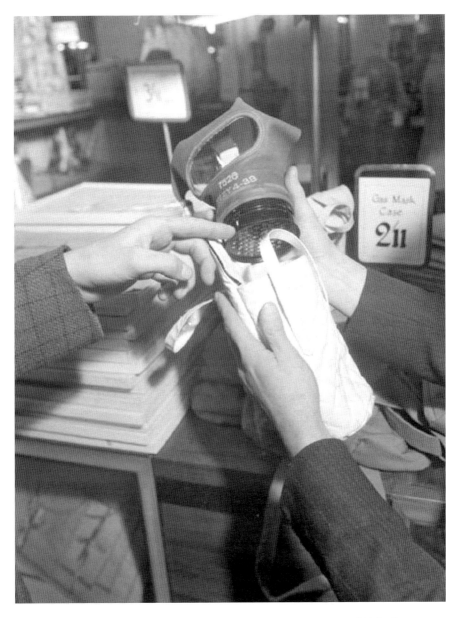

Selfridge's sold everything, including a selection of gas masks during World War II.

They gave him an ultimatum: he could either "retire" and relinquish all control of the business, or he would have to immediately repay the monies he owed to the company—about £100,000, plus another £250,000 that

Scaffolding covers the original section of the store during a 1957 renovation project.

he owed in back taxes to the Inland Revenue. He didn't have any choice. His fortunes were gone, long since squandered on pretty showgirls who stripped him of his money and his pride. Holmes offered him the mostly symbolic title of president and a tax-free salary of £6,000 per year for life. The store that he had built would go on without him, but even the name would reflect his ouster: the board immediately dropped the apostrophe, which indicated the possessive. Selfridge's was now Selfridges, and Harry no longer had a role.

Holmes later noted that Selfridge took the news stoically, but perhaps he didn't really believe what had happened. The next day, and for months afterward, he showed up at the store at his regular time and took the private lift to his office, where he sat quietly and stared out the window. The senior staff felt embarrassed and awkward. Everyone had assumed that he would quietly pack up and leave after his dismissal, but Harry showed no such inclination. Finally, they were forced to ask him to vacate, but they did offer him a small office in a building across the street. He accepted the gesture and continued his daily trek to Oxford Street for months, with nothing to do but sit in his chair and dream. By now, he was living with his daughter Rosalie and her husband, completely destitute and increasingly feeble. The fancy Rolls-Royce had long since been sold, and now his trips to the West End were by bus. He would carefully count out his coins for the driver and quietly ride until he was let off in front of the grand store that he had birthed. He would shuffle along the sidewalk, staring into the window displays or peering up at the roof. By this point, few people recognized him, and those who did were saddened by his threadbare attire and rambling mind. On one such trip, he was picked up in front of the store for vagrancy; the police were astounded to learn that the frail and shabby old man in their custody was indeed the legendary Harry Gordon Selfridge. The Earl of Oxford Street had been deposed, but his kingdom would live on without him.

THE DEATH OF A
MERCHANT PRINCE

When I die, I want it said of me that I dignified and ennobled commerce.
—Harry Gordon Selfridge

The winter of 1947 brought London to its knees. When the first gentle snowflakes began to fall on January 23, no one anticipated the misery that was forthcoming. The city had suffered greatly during World War II, and the subsequent months had done little to improve its lot. Wartime rationing continued and covered a vast array of necessities: meat, butter, lard, sugar, tea, cheese, soap, petrol and other goods could only be had in exchange for the meager ration tickets that people clutched like tenuous lifelines. Unemployment was rampant, and returning troops faced poverty and even homelessness due to the dire shortage of housing. Entire neighborhoods had been destroyed by bombing raids, and it seemed that no one had the materials or the strength to rebuild. The "Make Do and Mend" rallying cry that had once appealed to patriotic spirits now rang hollow to the exhausted and hungry populace. "We did win the war, didn't we?" they would ask one another with barely a trace of irony.

As the snow continued to fall, the temperature dropped precipitously. By January 29, Britain was experiencing the coldest weather it had had in more than fifty years, and the already scarce coal that fueled the country plunged to critically low levels. Gas supplies were cut to about a quarter of the normal pressure, and residents desperately wrapped themselves in layers of blankets as they huddled around anemic stoves and heaters. In response to the crisis, Minister of Fuel and Power Baron Shinwell cut off power to most industries in the region and announced that the use of residential electricity would be banned for five hours each day. Those who ignored the mandate faced stiff fines and possible jail time.

By mid-February, nearly 2 million people were unemployed due to the impact on industry. One woman noted that she couldn't bathe because there was no heat and the pipes were frozen, but it mattered little because she couldn't obtain soap either due to rationing. Another housewife complained that the precious bag of coal she had struggled to procure was filled with mostly slate and stone. "But at least we're not being bombed," she sighed. It was little consolation for a city whose emotional scars ran as deep as the physical. A first-time visitor wrote home and painted a bleak picture of what he was seeing at the time: "Public buildings [are] filthy and pitted with shrapnel scars running with pigeon dung. Bus tickets and torn newspapers blew down the streets; whole suburbs of private houses were peeling, cracking, their windows unwashed, their steps unswept, their gardens untended. [It is] a decaying, decrepit, sagging, rotten city."

Selfridges did not escape the pain that London was feeling. During the war, the store had been damaged by bombs, and the massive plate glass windows

A German bombing raid caused extensive damage to a section of the store in 1941.

Selfridge's simple grave, foreground, was separated from those of his wife, Rose, and mother, Lois, by the graves of two strangers.

were temporarily bricked over for safety. Now, with freedom at hand, the energy crisis forced the closure of the massive bargain basement, and the electric lights were switched off. The store was "terribly cold," according to Miss Mephan, the executive secretary, and rationing had made much of the inventory scarce. But perhaps the saddest moment came on May 8, 1947, when newspaper headlines cried out that department store magnate Harry Gordon Selfridge had died in his sleep that morning. He was ninety-one years old; of course, few newspapers reported that. Most claimed that he was eighty-nine or eighty-six or eighty-five, as no one really knew for sure. Harry had spun so many tales.

His memorial service was held one week later at St. Paul's Church. The chapel was filled with Selfridge's employees, who came to offer one last goodbye to their beloved "Chief." His family, which included his daughters and their husbands as well as his grandchildren, spoke of his passion for the store and his deep fondness for the staff. Among the floral arrangements—of course, Harry always loved his flowers—was a beautiful wreath of red and white roses from the surviving Dolly twin, Rosie. The card was signed "from Rosie and Jenny." Marshall Field's staff also remembered their long-ago colleague and sent their condolences along with an impressive wreath of roses and lilies. Reverend Colin Kerr eulogized Selfridge by comparing the imposing Oxford Street store to a self-made monument to the great man's life.

But by his death, he had precious little left to show for his spectacular existence. His treasured store had been wrenched from him and his vast

Selfridges decorations are legendary in London.

Christmas on Oxford Street.

The Selfridges Birmingham store opened in 2003. Its futuristic construction has won several architectural awards.

fortunes lost. Those he loved the most were gone. His brilliance had faded as new young kings of commerce set out to make their mark on the world. The showman who had once designed elaborate and extravagant displays

111

Walkway at the Selfridges Birmingham store at the Bullring shopping center.

to celebrate the milestones of others was now laid to rest in a simple dusty grave in a Highcliffe churchyard near his wife and his mother. The family couldn't afford a headstone. Selfridge had largely supported his daughters and their spouses, and without his fortune, they were all as poor as church mice. Harry couldn't even be buried in a plot adjacent to Rose or Lois; he is separated from them by two decrepit, unmarked graves. The simple headstone that was added later reads, "In Loving Memory Harry Gordon

Snow White and the Seven Dwarfs join Santa at Selfridges for a Christmas celebration.

Selfridge 1857–1947." Ironically, even in death Harry vainly managed to shave a year off his age; his actual birth year was 1856.

Of course, the grand store lived on and even thrived. In 1951, the Oxford Street store was sold to the Lewis's chain of department stores, which had earlier purchased Selfridge's Provincial Stores in the 1940s. In 1965, the Sears Group bought out Lewis's holdings and expanded with three more Selfridges locations, in Birmingham, Manchester and Trafford Centre. Finally, Canada's Galen Weston purchased the chain for £598 million in 2003 and has spent a great deal of money on renovating and improving the Oxford Street store, including the reopening of the rooftop gardens and entertainment. Since then, Selfridges has been voted "the best department store in the world" on three consecutive occasions by the Intercontinental Group of Department Stores, an industry association.

Harry once joked, "When I die I want a round coffin, so that I can turn easily in my grave if I want to." If he could see how his empire has grown and thrived, he would most likely be twirling in delight.

MARSHALL FIELD'S
TEA ROOM RECIPES

O n the opening day of Selfridge's new restaurant at Field's, the menu included chicken potpie, chicken salad, corned beef hash, orange punch served in an orange shell and Field's Rose Punch, which was vanilla ice cream blended with a rose cordial. The recipes here were developed by Selfridge and his staff to delight the customers and offer them a hearty repast so that they would have the stamina to continue shopping the great store. If you serve these, don't forget to place a red rose on the plate—that was Harry's signature touch.

MRS. HERING'S FAMOUS ORIGINAL CHICKEN POTPIE

Pie Dough:
1½ cups flour, sifted
½ teaspoon salt
8 tablespoons (1 stick) cold unsalted butter, cut into small pieces
¼ cup vegetable shortening (Crisco), chilled
3 to 4 tablespoons ice water

Chicken:
1 frying chicken, approximately 3 pounds
1 carrot
1 celery stalk
1 small onion, halved
2 teaspoons salt

After Selfridge proved that shoppers would welcome an in-store restaurant, Field's quickly expanded the idea. The store soon boasted seven different eateries.

Filling:
6 tablespoons unsalted butter
1 large onion, diced (about 1¼ cups)
3 carrots, thinly sliced on the diagonal
3 celery stalks, thinly sliced on the diagonal
½ cup flour
1½ cups milk
1 teaspoon chopped fresh thyme leaves

¼ cup sherry
¾ cup frozen green peas, thawed
2 tablespoons fresh parsley, minced
2 teaspoons salt
½ teaspoon freshly ground black pepper

1 egg whisked with 1 tablespoon water for glazing

To prepare pie dough:
Combine flour, salt and butter in the bowl of a food processor and pulse five times to combine. Add the shortening and pulse a few more times, until the dough resembles coarse cornmeal. Transfer to a bowl and sprinkle with 3 tablespoons ice water. Stir and then press together to form a ball. If the dough won't come together, add more water as needed. Flatten the dough into a disk. Cover in plastic wrap and refrigerate for at least 30 minutes or up to two days before rolling.

To cook chicken:
Combine chicken, carrot, celery, onion and salt in a large stockpot. Add cold water as needed to cover and bring to a boil over high heat. Decrease the heat to low and simmer for 45 minutes. Remove chicken, reserving liquid, and transfer chicken to a plate to allow it to cool. Increase the heat to high and boil the remaining broth for 20 minutes to reduce and concentrate. Strain the broth through a fine-mesh sieve and discard the vegetables. Reserve broth. When cool enough to handle, pull the chicken meat from the bones and shred into bite-size pieces.

To prepare filling:
Place a large saucepan over medium heat and add butter. When the butter is melted, add the onion, carrots and celery and cook, stirring occasionally for 10 minutes, until the onion is soft and translucent. Add the flour and cook, stirring constantly, for 1 minute. Slowly whisk in the milk and 2½ cups of reserved chicken broth. Decrease the heat to low and simmer, stirring often, for 10 minutes. Add the chicken meat, thyme, sherry, peas, parsley, salt and pepper and stir well. Taste and adjust seasoning as necessary. Divide the filling among six 12-ounce potpie tins or individual ramekins.

To assemble and bake:
Preheat oven to 400 degrees Fahrenheit. Next, place chilled dough on a floured surface and roll out to ¼-inch thick. Cut into six rounds about 1 inch larger than the circumference of the tins or ramekins. Carefully place a dough round over each filled dish. Turn the edges of the dough back under itself and flute the edges with a fork. Cut a 1-inch slit in the top of each pie. Brush the dough with the egg and water mixture to glaze and seal the top, which will give the final product an attractive finish. Line a baking sheet with foil to catch the liquid that will bubble over and place pies on baking sheet and bake for 25 minutes or until the pastry is golden and the filling bubbles. Serve hot. Makes six individual pies or one large potpie.

MRS. HERING'S QUICK CHICKEN POTPIE (EASY VERSION)

1 sheet frozen puff pastry dough, thawed
3 tablespoons chicken fat or butter
¼ cup flour
2 cups chicken broth
salt and pepper to taste
12-ounce package cooked chicken breast meat, cut or torn into bite-sized strips
¼ cup petite frozen peas, thawed
¼ cup diced cooked carrots
½ teaspoon dried thyme

Preheat oven to 450 degrees Fahrenheit. Using potpie tins or individual ramekins, cut circles from the puff pastry to slightly overlap the tops of the dishes. Melt fat or butter in a medium pan and add flour, stirring constantly for about 1 minute. Add broth, whisking until smooth. Heat to a boil and cook 1 to 2 minutes until thickened. Season with salt and pepper to taste. Add cooked chicken, peas, carrots and thyme. Heat through and then divide the mixture among the ramekins. Top with a pastry round, tuck the edges in and flute with fork. Cut a one-inch slit in each pie to vent. Place on foil-lined baking sheet and bake 20 to 25 minutes until puffy and golden. Serve hot. Makes two individual pies.

Marshall Field's Corned Beef Hash

3 pounds cooked, trimmed brisket corned beef
2 pounds cooked potatoes
½ ounce grated onions
dash of pepper
½ quart milk
salt to taste
1 ounce butter

Grind corned beef with ⅜-inch blade of meat grinder. Next, chop cooked potatoes. For best results, cook potatoes in advance and refrigerate overnight. Combine corned beef, potatoes, onion, pepper and milk together thoroughly but lightly in small quantities. Taste and add salt if necessary. Fill casseroles with 8 ounces of the mixture. Brush top with butter and bake in a 350-degree oven 10 to 15 minutes or until hot through and golden brown. Serves 8 to 12.

Marshall Field's Chicken Salad

For dressing:
½ cup mayonnaise
¼ cup sour cream
1 tablespoon Dijon mustard
1 teaspoon sugar
¼ teaspoon salt
¼ teaspoon white pepper
2½ teaspoons lemon juice

For salad:
1½ cups shredded cooked boneless skinless
  chicken breasts
½ cup celery, finely chopped
2 tablespoons green onions, finely chopped
¼ cup pecans, toasted and chopped
¼ cup green seedless grapes, halved (optional)

Mix all dressing ingredients together in large bowl. Add chicken, celery, green onion, pecans and grapes (if using). Mix well. Cover and refrigerate for at least 2 hours. Serves 2 to 4.

Modern-day Selfridges boasts a Starbucks store.

MARSHALL FIELD'S ROSE PUNCH

Although the original recipe hasn't been found, here's a quick and delicious method for making rose cordial. Field's served this lightly blended with softened vanilla ice cream. There are also rose liqueurs on the market if you prefer a more "spirited" version.

1 cup sugar
1 cup cold water
about 1 cup rose petals
honey to taste (optional)

Place sugar and water into a nonstick pan over medium-high heat and bring to a boil. Turn the heat to low and add the rose petals. Stir constantly until the sugar dissolves completely, approximately 3 to 5 minutes. The longer you boil the mixture, the thicker it will be when cooled. Remove from heat and allow to cool to room temperature. Once cooled, pour into a clean glass jar that can be tightly sealed and store in the refrigerator.

Index

E

Ely Cathedral 43

F

feminist movement 22, 81
Field, Leiter and Company 20, 27
Field, Leonard 15, 20, 28
Field, Marshall 15, 20, 24, 25, 26, 27,
28, 29, 30, 31, 32, 34, 35, 38,
39, 40, 41, 43, 44, 45, 47, 53,
54, 55, 57, 58, 64, 65, 76, 81
"Silent Marsh" 28, 34
Fleming, J.M. 31, 32, 34, 39
flu pandemic (1918) 86, 92
Furness, Thelma 96

G

Gerrard, Teddie 74
Gilbert, Ransom & Knapp 17
Glyn, Elinor 89
Goldsman, Edward 71, 74, 75
Good Wife's Cook Book, The 82
Great Chicago Fire 28, 49

H

Harrod's 85
Harrose Hall 44
Hering, Sarah 35, 36
H.G. Selfridge and Company (Chicago)
59
Highcliffe Castle 91, 93, 112
Holmes, H. Andrew 100, 102, 105
Honeycombe, Gordon 17, 100
Honore, Bertha 28

K

Kerr, Reverend Colin 109
King George V 80
Kit Kat Club 93

L

Lake Geneva, Wisconsin 44, 47, 63
Lake Shore Drive (Chicago) 31, 43, 47
Lake Street (Chicago) 23, 27, 50
Leiter, Joseph 55
Leiter, Levi 26, 27, 28, 29, 30, 31, 49,
54, 55
Lenglen, Suzanne 100
London Building Act 67, 71
Loomis, Peter "Burr" 15, 16
Low, Archibald Montgomery 84

M

MacLeish, Andrew 61
Mandel Brothers 53, 54
Marshall Field & Company 31, 34, 36,
37, 38, 43, 44, 47, 49, 50, 58,
59, 64, 67, 71, 73, 81, 109
Maugham, William Somerset 90
Mayer, David 47, 48, 49, 52, 53, 54,
55, 57, 58
Morgan, J.P. 64
Musker, John 70, 84

N

Naval Academy, Annapolis, Maryland
16, 17
Netcher, Irving 97
newspapers, advertising 15, 16, 39,
74, 85

O

Oppenheimer, William 71

P

Palmer and Selover Company 19
Palmer House 28
Palmer, Milton 26
Palmer, Potter 22, 23, 24, 25, 26, 27,
28, 65
Pavlova, Anna 89
Pirie, John T. 59, 61

ABOUT THE AUTHOR

Gayle Soucek is an author and freelance editor with more than a dozen books to her credit, including *Marshall Field's, Carson's* and several other titles with The History Press. Her interests include a wide range of subjects, from history to ornithology, science and true crime. She is a lifelong Chicagoan and Blackhawks hockey fan, residing in the far northwest suburbs with her photographer husband, dogs, parrots, reptiles and one very laidback cat.